གཞན་སྟོང་དབུ་མ་ཆེན་མོ། འཇིགས་བྲལ་ལྷ་ཡི་རྒྱལ་ང་།

The Divine Victory Drum of
The Great Middle Way

*The eighteen unique qualities of
the all-knowing, victorious Jonangpa textual tradition,
along with the associated view, doctrines, practices
and the clearing of objections.*

by Shar Khentrul Jamphel Lodrö

༸ར་མཁན་སྤྲུལ་འཇམ་དཔལ་བློ་གྲོས།

Dzokden Publications
SAN FRANCISCO, USA

DZOKDEN PUBLICATIONS

3436 Divisadero Street
San Francisco, California
USA 94123

This work was produced by Dzokden Publications, a not-for-profit organisation dedicated to the manifestation of peace and harmony in this world through the creation and distribution of high quality educational materials related to the profound teachings of Kalachakra.

For more information, please visit:
dzokden.org

Copyright © 2020 Shar Khentrul Jamphel Lodrö

Author: Shar Khentrul Jamphel Lodrö
Translator: Ives Waldo
Editor: Ven. Tenpai Gyaltsen

Paperback : 978-1-7349115-0-3
E-book : 978-1-7349115-1-0

Library of Congress Control Number: 2020907793

Acknowledgements

Khentrul Rinpoché would like to thank all those who helped to make this book available in the English language. In particular, Ives Waldo for his wonderful translation, Tenpai Gyaltsen for editing the material, and all those who offered feedback and helped polish the final manuscript. May the service you have given become the cause for all sentient beings to realize the profound truth of their innate buddha-nature.

Contents

Preface — VII
Homage and Aspiration to Compose — XI

1. Introduction to Zhentong Madhyamaka — 1
2. The Uncommon Ground, Path and Result — 19
3. The Seven Kinds of Misconception — 25
4. The Eighteen Unique Qualities of the Jonang View — 49
5. Clearing Away Faults that Deprecate Zhentong — 123
6. Excerpts from the Textual Tradition — 151

Conclusion — 161

About the Author — 165

— *Kunkhyen Dolpopa Sherab Gyaltsen* —
The Great Pioneer of Zhentong Madhyamaka in Tibet

Preface

There are four reasons why I felt that this book needed to be written. Firstly, the tradition of Zhentong Madhyamaka is widely recognized and experienced by the lineage masters of all of the Tibetan traditions as being the view and doctrine which most clearly illuminates the very essence of the Buddha's teachings. In accordance with this tradition, sutra and tantra are found to be completely non-contradictory and when dealing with the two truths, it is a most effective method for achieving liberation from conceptual fixation to the views of eternalism and nihilism. It also appears to have an extraordinary capacity to arouse the mind of enlightenment, bodhicitta—the mind that strives to bring ultimate benefit to sentient beings while also achieving one's own ultimate liberation.

Therefore I thought, "Wouldn't it be wonderful if more people knew about this tradition and were able to realize it?" Inspired in this way and recognising that these teachings are more valuable than the most precious of jewels, I therefore decided to write this text even though it is possible that I may offend those with fixated or biased views.

Secondly, throughout Tibet and also in many other parts of the world, the legendary kingdom of Shambhala is held to be a particularly precious pure land. For many, there is nothing more important than to take rebirth there. They know that through such a birth, they will definitely experience the genuine peace and harmony that comes from knowing the natural state of all phenomena.

However, achieving this result can only occur in reliance upon the Kalki Kings of Shambhala turning the wheel of dharma for the Age of Perfection. While some people are aware of this in general, they do not understand the specific reasons why this age is necessary, nor how it should be established. Since this is the principal focus of the teachings of the victorious Jonang tradition, I think it is very important that it is clearly understood.

Thirdly, throughout the world and especially in Tibet, thousands upon thousands of people have received the great empowerment of Kalachakra. It is widely known to be a most incomparably exalted, profound and complete Dharma. However, most people aren't fully aware or do not understand that only the Jonang are the principal holders of the complete textual and practice tradition of this system. This is largely due to the fact that they have historically avoided getting involved in politics and instead chose to stay in remote places where they could focus on practicing the Profound Path of Vajra Yoga in reliance on the view of Zhentong Madhyamaka.

However, due to these teachings being preserved only within the Jonang Tradition, many people in and outside of Tibet are not aware of them, nor do they understand them. If this trend continues, then these teachings are in danger of disappearing. Such a loss would be incredibly unfortunate not only for Tibet but also for the entire world. Therefore, it is my hope that by writing about how to embrace the view of Zhentong Madhyamaka, I will help to establish the limitless wealth of this incredibly precious treasure of the glorious and victorious Jonang tradition.

Finally, for the reasons stated above, so few people are even aware of the existence of the Jonang, let alone their profound view of Zhentong. Of the few that are aware, due to centuries of suppression that has continued up to recent times, there are many who think that the Jonang are a degenerate school of little import. Some even believe that the Jonang are completely non-existent. The fact that these views permeate modern Tibetan culture is extremely tragic.

I consider this extraordinary tradition of learning and practice to be established by some of the greatest minds that Tibet has ever produced. It is truly a great and profound treasure for this world. If we do not master it, then there can be no greater loss. For this reason, feeling a sense of great urgency to preserve this tradition in Tibet and also share it with the world, I have written this text.

Understanding these reasonings, one may ask, "How did it happen that something so valuable could be neglected for so long?" Then I would answer that due to oppressive political views perpetuated over many centuries, these teachings were forgotten by the general public. Since the details of this history have been explained by many very intelligent people, I do not feel the need to discuss them further here.

However, even now, there have been a number of recent setbacks. Due to being short-sighted and dominated by attachment, aversion, and ignorance, there are those who continue to be swept away by the cycle of existence. Lost in the pursuit of their own ambition and desire, they allow their conceptual thoughts to consume them and therefore disregard the rights of others.

The natural decency which is common to all people in this world is now thickly wrapped in a sheath of shameless indecency and self-obsession. If we continue to act in this way, future generations will look back at this time with remorse and embarrassment at the way society has been driven by such greed and self-indulgent behavior.

With these teachings, we have the opportunity to immediately wake up from this deep slumber of ignorant behavior. Therefore, for the sake of our future generations, we must never again allow our minds to be infected by such noxious maladies. To this end, I have written this so that we may become masters of the hidden jewel of Tibet. By virtue of this effort, I pray for an auspicious time in which this treasure of the Zhentong Madhyamaka is enjoyed as the shared legacy of all people in this world.

Khentrul Rinpoche
Shanghai, China 2018

— Kyabje Lama Lobsang Trinlé —
My root lama who taught me Zhentong Madhyamaka

Homage and Aspiration to Compose

Lord of Secrets pleasing those with sagacious mind and a great attitude; Blessed with the display of major marks and having the activity of the Medicine Buddha; Lord of Dharma who manifests the ten signs of empty-form; Most precious Lama Lobsang Trinlé, you are always in my heart.

Second Buddha in the Land of Snow Mountains; Prophesied by "Arising, I will hoist the victory banner of Dharma!"; Confirming the exalted teachings of the sutras and tantras; Dolpopa Sherab Gyaltsen, the victorious Lord of this world.

With the nature of mind, he reveals the complete and profound dharma; Through non-conceptual self-aware primordial wisdom, He conquers the speech of logicians with liberating confidence. I pay homage to the lineage lamas who flow from Jetsun Taranatha and so forth.

The one who clears all degeneration when relied upon; The lord of increasing qualities, like the waxing moon. In whom sage-like wisdom, virtue and so forth are complete. The spiritual friend Yonten Sangpo, I will remember you always until the end of samsara.

Absolute primordial nature, free from beginning or end; Pure self of the exalted buddhas, spontaneously self-existent; For sentient beings, Buddha-nature is the meaning of the ground; In reality, it is the inseparability of ground and result. I pay homage to that!

The absolute self of the ultimate truth body, That which is empty of the two selves that are suitable to be refuted; The absolute self of the ultimate form body, That which is the perfection of the two accumulations that are already established.

Free from all elaborations of refutation or proof, The faultless way things are is the absolute truth body. Without any contradiction or inconsistency, It is the pure and lucid self of reality, Buddhahood.

That which remains after the refutation of establishment, Is the ground of great emptiness. That which remains within the empty void of refutation is the supreme affirmation. Free from the refutations or proof of the relative, it is the expanse of great proof. The absolute affirmation possessing all supreme aspects;

Transcending causes and conditions, the primordially permanent phenomena; Not arising in dependence on others, it is self-arisen and spontaneously present. Not the sphere of words and concepts, beyond speech, thought and expression. I pay homage to this great purity of non-thought which is never the subject of mere intellectual analysis.

As the absolute Buddha-nature is empty of everything other, how could it be empty of itself? All of the relative phenomena which make up samsara are deceptive phenomena, empty of self and other. Not known by immature beings, or known only a little, this truth is known fully by the wise. The true and authentic view can thus be distinguished as being realized completely, only partially or not at all.

The vajra nature is without the change of waxing and waning. Beyond speech, thought and expression, it possesses the supreme of all aspects. The expanse of great emptiness is that which transcends describable emptiness. May that which is ineffable terminate all mistaken paths of expression.

PREFACE

Coming forth from the mental expanse of the Second Buddha, the Omniscient One Dolpopa, it is without finite depth or limit. Even though this true meaning may irritate the ears of the immature, it is only spoken from the heart of compassion; therefore, please help me!

Even though inferior and devious minds do not care whether the teachings are true or authentic, by the power of the Conquerors of the ten directions and my sincere aspiration, may this text be a cause for only benefit and happiness!

— Shakyamuni Buddha —
The root source for the teachings on Buddha-nature.

CHAPTER ONE

Introduction to Zhentong Madhyamaka

In accordance with the textual tradition of the Great Jonangpa, the Omniscient One possessing the Four Reliances Dolpopa Sherab Gyaltsen, I shall now teach the ultimate view of Zhentong Madhyamaka that brings forth the definitive meaning of all sutras and tantras. This is the most exalted of all views and doctrines of the snowy land of Tibet.

There are many reasons for making such a statement. To give one, for more than a thousand years the lineage masters of the Jonang tradition have single-pointedly brought forth the power of the natural state of reality as a result of practicing the Profound Path of Vajra Yoga, the intended meaning of the Kalachakra Tantra. As is widely known by a great many unbiased scholar-practitioners, their attainments have arisen from the confidence of authentic realization.

Among the holders of the Kalachakra tradition, the practice of the Six Yogas has been famed from the time that the tantra was first transmitted. However, from the thirteenth century onwards, it has been most closely associated with the Jonang practitioners. Their completely perfect view is that of Zhentong—the Great Middle Way of Other Emptiness.

Even though this is certainly true, this view is not held exclusively by the Jonangpas. Among all of the great chariots of the eight practice lineages that made their way into the snowy land of Tibet, this view has also been held by many highly regarded masters from other traditions. Regardless of the common views associated with their respective traditions, these most esteemed scholar-practitioners were its advocates and they expressed great respect and admiration for Zhentong Madhyamaka.

To name just a few of them as examples, we can begin with the early translation school—the Nyingma. This view was held by the Lord of Victorious Ones, the Great Longchen Rabjam (1308-1364). Likewise, the great Terton of Mindrolling, Gyurme Dorjé (1308-1364), Getsé Mahapandita, Gyurme Tsewang Chokdrub (1761-1829) and Khathog Rigdzin Tsewang Norbu (1698-1755) were all greatly inspired by the teachings on Zhentong. More recently, Ju Mipham Jamyang Namgyal Gyatso (1846-1912) also advocated Zhentong. In addition, Sechen Gyaltsap (1871-1926), the Great Khenpo Gangshar (1925-1980) and others did so as well. In brief, among the Nyingma there does not seem to exist any great masters who did not highly appreciate the teachings on Zhentong.

Very recently we can also see the example of the accomplished vidyadhara Chatral Sangye Dorjé (1913-2015), and the most revered of his followers, the great khenpo of Nub Zur Jigmé Phuntsok (1933-2004). Among their students, there is also the supremely competent elder Khenpo Tsultrim Lodrö (b. 1962) who has powerful knowledge of both the traditional and modern teachings, the latest emanation of Kathog Rigzin Chenpo, Padma Wangchen (b. 1973), the great khenpo Dampa Chimé Rigdzin (1922-2002) and other great khenpos of Larung Gar. There are indeed many more who are knowledgeable of the final turning and greatly appreciate the Zhentong teachings, but these will suffice for now.

Among the practitioners of the Kagyu tradition, there are many scholar-practitioners, such as the Protector of Beings, the Third Karmapa Rangjung Dorjé (1284-1339). In fact, most of the subsequent reincarnations in the line of the Gyalwang Karmapas have also appreciated this view such as the seventh Karmapa Chödrak Gyatso (1454-1506), the eighth the eminent scholar Mikyo Dorjé (1507-1554), the tenth Thekchok Dorjé (1797-1867), the thirteenth Dudul Dorjé (1733-1797), the fifteenth Kakhyab Dorjé (1871-1922), and the sixteenth Rangjung Rigpé Dorjé (1924-1981) as well as the four fathers and sons of Kamtsang Monastery.

In addition, there was Gö Lotsawa Zhonnu Pal (1392-1481), the great Tsurphu Jamyang (1424-1482), the Shamarpa Chennga Chokyi Drakpa (1453-1524) and the great Jamgön Kongtrul Lodrö Thaye (1813-1899). In the line of Tai Situ, there was the great pandit Situ Chokyi Jungné (1700-1774), the eighth Pema Nyinjé Wangpo (1813-1899) and the eleventh-Pema Wangchuk Gyalpo (1886-1952). Also, there was Beri Khyentse (b. 1947), Lhagsam Tenpe Gyaltsen (c. 1800), Karma Ngelek (1700 - 1768), the great khenpo of Palpung Tashi Ozer (1836-1910), and the protector Drikung Jigten Gönpo, Yongdzin Do Gangkar (1143-1217).

In more recent times, the current tutor of His Holiness the Gyalwang Karmapa, Khenchen Thrangu Rinpoché (b. 1933), as well as Khenchen Tsultrim Gyatso (b. 1934), the vajra master Tenga Rinpoché (1932-2012) and many others have also taught just this.

Among the Sakyapas, there was the Glorious Pandita of Sakya, Shakya Chokden (1428-1507), the erudite Lhundrub Gyatso (1523-1596), and the principal founder of the rimé movement in the east, Jamyang Khyentse Wangpo (1820-1892).

Within the Geluk Tradition of Ganden Monastery, there were the close disciples of Lord Tsongkhapa: the gentle-voiced Lord of Dharma the great Tashi Palden (1379-1449), the precious tulku of Drakar Monastery Gyaltsen Sangpo of Gungru (1383-1450), the third in the line of Jamyang Shepa Kelsang Thubten Wangchuk (1856-1916), the teacher of Zhang Tenpa Gyatso (1825-1897) and many others who were hidden practitioners of these teachings.

Perhaps most notably, many within the line of the Dalai Lamas are said to have had a secret connection with these teachings and are known to have analyzed it. In this present century, one need look no further than the great fourteenth Dalai Lama, His Holiness Tenzin Gyatso. While giving the extremely secret transmissions of the eight great practice lineages to the Geluk practitioners of the lower tantric college of Sera in Lhasa, the Dalai Lama is reported to have given teachings on Zhentong. Whatever else may have been said during those transmissions, when it came time to practice the Six Vajra Yogas of Kalachakra, he is reported to have told his students to defer to the Jonangpas since except for them, there was no other trustworthy source to rely on. He also said that when one is studying the Six Limbed Practice, it is the same situation and there is nothing else to be done other than what is in accord with the Jonang teachings.

Then, on another occasion, when speaking about independent establishment, he taught that when the emptiness of empty-forms are taken as the object of meditation, those forms are realized to exist naturally and that they remain in one's experience even after one has realized emptiness. At that time, empty-forms are established by both logical refutations of the defiled relative other than itself and the establishment as the experience of the undefiled ultimate. Not being something that arises interdependently from incidental conditions, empty-form is a gradual shining forth of primordial luminosity in emptiness that arises due to the power of a yogin's practice.

Furthermore, he has previously recommended the teachings of Taktsang Lotsawa (1405-1477) as being quite good on this subject, as well as the commentary on the general meaning of the Kalachakra tantra that was written by the learned and accomplished Norsang Gyatso (1423-1513). He has said during teachings to Geluk practitioners:

> *The meaning of "independent" here should be understood in detail depending on these. If one makes careful distinctions, when one is engaged in this meditation, even though there are many debates around the intention of the Jonangpas, there should be no doubt that the naturally existing ultimate and the enlightened experience which remains after the experiential realization of emptiness are both very important key points that need to be taken into account.*

Echoing his points, the great non-sectarian master and khenpo of Larung Gar Tsultrim Lodrö has said:

> *When taking into account all of these Kalachakra practices, they are so extensive that it is difficult for everyone to complete. Moreover, if the continuity of the higher yogic practices are interrupted, then the many techniques of working with channels, subtle essences and wind energies become considerably more complicated. Since these must exist in order to achieve the completion of Kalachakra, they are found among the Nyingma practitioners of Kalachakra as well as in the Jonangpas. However, while there were formerly many Nyingmas who upheld these teachings, nowadays there are only a few. This pattern is similar for many of the other Dharma traditions.*

Also:

> *Not only are the Jonangpa teachings entirely in accord with the direct experience of the meaning of the Buddha's words in the final turning, but there is also not even a half-syllable that is added. Without the Jonang, we Tibetans cannot properly and completely elucidate the meaning of the three turnings. I am always thinking like this. If the Buddha-dharma is like an eight-petalled lotus, without the teachings of the Jonang, it would be like there was one petal missing.*

What all of this demonstrates is that many straightforward and unbiased Dharma Lords have recognized that the intended meaning of the Jonang teachings are profoundly significant. The fact that so many of the great minds of Tibet have expressed such praise for the Jonang view and doctrines is a testament to this.

In general, I believe that we must remember that we are all followers of a single teacher, Lord Buddha. By remembering this, then we avoid getting lost in a mind of mutual alienation that sees all of the different schools of Buddhism as completely unrelated and impossible to unite. By sharing our ideologies, we should not be afraid to engage in the mutual study of each others' views and doctrines. If we fail to do so, then by not accurately understanding the perspective of others, we will be doomed to abide in ignorance. That in itself would go against the essential purpose of why the Buddha turned the wheel of Dharma—to exhaust all ignorance. There is also the danger that the sanghas of the ten directions will have an incomplete refuge in the Dharma. Therefore, I can see no reason why we should not be able to reconcile the incompatibilities between our views and doctrines.

Within our textual traditions and practices, some aspects may be seen as less essential, and perhaps regarded as optional details which provide differences in style of presentation. However, the foundation of our views and doctrines—their common goal of peace and harmony—are necessarily one and the same.

How is this so? Consider our brothers and sisters of the southern lineages of the foundational vehicle. They are all of the family of those to be tamed by the study and practice of the Buddha's first turning of the Wheel of Dharma. That turning is the very foundation of the Buddha's teachings. Since all those who call themselves Buddhists are aware of these teachings, they form the root by which we can all reconcile our discordant views.

For our brothers and sisters of the eastern lineages of the mahayana vehicle, on the basis of the essential meaning of the first turning, they also add the study and practice of the teachings of the middle and third turnings. Among these Buddhists, while a few have complete knowledge of the sutras of the middle turning, all of them have at least a rough idea of the four noble truths. This is an indication that there is a common thread that connects them with the southern lineages.

The doctrines of the Tibetan lineages of the vajra vehicle appear to be very different with respect to the way monks dress, their conduct, liturgies, practices, the depictions of deities and so forth. However, this appearance is actually misleading since the ground or root of their views and doctrines, their discipline and so forth, are completely concordant with the other lineages.

INTRODUCTION TO ZHENTONG

Within the doctrines of the Tibetan lineages, practitioners have at least some awareness of the intended meaning of the first turning. They are versed in its textual tradition of personal liberation and they practice in accordance with the vinaya. They also have an extensive textual tradition related to the sutra teachings of the middle and final turnings. However, unlike the other lineages, they also have an extensive tradition of the study and practice of Buddhist tantra.

Due to relying on the skilful means of both sutra and tantra, those who practice within the Tibetan lineages come to recognize that the definitive meaning of both sets of teachings are ultimately the same. While there are numerous Dharma lineages that exist in Tibet, each with its own profound textual tradition of sutra and tantra, all of them are rooted in the three turnings of the Wheel of Dharma. There are none that fall outside these teachings.

It is widely known that from among the Tibetan traditions, the madhyamaka philosophy is considered supreme. However, within the Tibetan doctrines of madhyamaka, we can speak of two schools of thought—*rangtong* (self emptiness) and *zhentong* (other emptiness). Everything can be included in these two. Therefore it is very important to learn how to distinguish between rangtong and zhentong. Surprisingly though, while a great many people are at least partially familiar with the rangtong interpretation of madhyamaka, very few understand the meaning of zhentong. For this reason, in order to elucidate the meaning and distinctions of these two, I will temporarily put aside the more subtle points that are found in texts and instead focus on the basic principles involved so that they may be clearly and easily understood.

It is a common misconception that the ultimate meaning of these two is very hard to understand. This has given rise to a great deal of debate over the centuries. Even now, it is hard to find anyone who has come to a final conclusion. In my humble opinion, the reason for this is that historically, from the very beginning, the basic meaning of the terms "rangtong" and "zhentong" were misunderstood.

This confusion stems from people trying to fit these terms into the previously established tenets of existing textual traditions, instead of actually relying on their fundamental meanings. By projecting onto these terms all sorts of additional philosophical meanings, the direct meaning of the terms became clouded and thus harder to understand. This fault can be avoided by not focusing on projections. Instead we should focus on the direct, fundamental meaning of these words. When we grasp that meaning, then we will see how all of the doctrines expound upon and provide ornamentation to that meaning. This makes things much easier to understand.

In keeping with this strategy, I will present the subjects and terms used by these schools as well as their fundamental positions from the perspective of how the meaning is directly experienced. This is important to be aware of as you read, since the whole point of familiarising ourselves with these philosophies is to know them directly in our experience.

In general, all terms have the nature of being conventions. They have a fundamental meaning in relation to how they are used within a worldly context. If we focus on what each convention is trying to communicate, then it will be relatively easy to understand them.

Let's start with the word "tong", which in english means "empty". When we say "Y is empty of X", it means that some phenomena X is non-existent within some other phenomena Y. In such a relationship, Y is called "the ground of emptiness." That is the essence of these words. It doesn't have to be more complicated than that.

Then we have the word "rang", which is translated as "itself". This term is referring to the essence of a phenomena, that which is its own being, or that very thing. There is no trick here. Just think about the common meaning that is understood by everyone in your own culture.

When we say "rangtong", we are saying "empty of itself". That means that some phenomena or something that is knowable is said to exist conventionally, but from the viewpoint of the ultimate truth—the way things actually are—that phenomena or knowable object *itself* (rang nyid) is empty of its own *intrinsic essence* (rang gi ngo bor). The intrinsic essence is non-existent in the knowable object.

Such a self-empty phenomena can only exist as a relative truth. It does not fulfill the criteria or function of something which exists as the ultimate truth. If you ask why not, it is because such phenomena, when not examined or analyzed intellectually, are seen to exist in ordinary life arising as mere appearances within our experience. Conventionally, we can say they exist as they appear, because they are able to fulfill expected causal functions.

However, all such relative, causal objects are said to be non-existent in ultimate truth or the ultimate way things are, due to the fact that when we analyze our assertions of their existence, we find that the assertion cannot be established, leaving only the mere appearances which are experienced. While these merely imputed phenomena definitely do not exist from the perspective of the primordial wisdom of self-awareness, they don't even exist within the conceptual mind of logic and reasoning. Even in modern science, we can see that when we analyze material particles with technology, we can't find anything substantial there. Eventually all matter dissolves back into the quantum field. This leads us to the conclusion that all of the conventional entities of relative truth are empty of their own essence in ultimate truth. Even the concept of "relative truth" when analyzed is not found. When we think about these ideas even just a little in a careful and detailed way, then it is quite understandable. Unfortunately, most people don't think like this.

Instead, all phenomena of sights and sounds appear to us to be real things, truly existing from their own side, just as they appear. Due to this fundamental delusion, we take on the aspect of a deluded sentient being. In a universe where there is no self, we grasp a self of individuals and a self of phenomena. Even though all of these relative phenomena can be demonstrated to not inherently exist in reality, due to our continual grasping onto things as real, we fixate on relative objects that do not correspond with reality. There is a mismatch between the mode of being and the mode of abiding.

As a result of this we cycle helplessly in samsara again and again, necessarily experiencing suffering due to our fixation on conceptualized appearances. The "root of samsara" is just this. There is nothing else that we need to look for. The rangtong view which logically establishes the self-emptiness of the delusive relative is fundamental to all understandings of madhyamaka philosophy. This includes Zhentong Madhyamaka, where it is taught for the specific purpose of clearing away the many sufferings of samsara such as sickness, demonic attacks and other calamities. When we clearly understand rangtong, then we can abandon all of these deluded limitations and ultimately attain the liberation which abides in the experience of immutable great bliss or simply "immutable bliss" as it is known in the texts of the unsurpassed tantras.

If we focus now on understanding this unchanging liberation, we can find many explanations in the individual doctrines. Many of them identify "liberation" as the mere negation of the two obscurations. If we then ask if that sort of liberation is empty or not, then we find many answers which are not really consistent or stable.

Some proponents of rangtong say that emptiness is an intellectual understanding that is set aside from experience, such as "the absence of the afflictive states of mind which is separate from the experience of the relative." However, such an intellectual form of emptiness could never abide within one's own experience as the realization that apprehends reality as bliss and luminosity. Since the self-emptiness that must be grasped and labeled by a conceptual mind as some theoretical thing that exists "beyond the scope of experience", it is established to be non-existent. That which is unreal then has nowhere else to go.

If we take something that is non-existent to be the ultimate way things are, then "attaining" such a thing is completely ruled out other than perhaps within a thought experiment. It is contradictory to say that the nature of reality is non-existence. Even in regular language, this is obviously wrong.

The ultimate is by definition the nature of reality. Therefore, of all the subjects we should be concerned with, it is definitely foremost. However, there is no one who consciously wants to strive for and attain something that is non-existent. It simply doesn't happen. Even if someone could have that idea, striving for something that doesn't exist is meaningless.

Therefore, while the reasonings which establish the concept of the ultimate and the concept of liberation to be self-empty may have great provisional benefit by allowing us to remove the attachment that fixates onto a self of persons and a self of phenomena, if we characterize the emptiness of the ultimate buddha-nature as being the emptiness of true existence and proclaim that it is non-existent, then liberation becomes meaningless. Even though it is very important for all Buddhists to fully understand the absence of self, we must be careful not to overextend the methodology.

Zhentongpas agree with rangtongpas that all relative phenomena are empty of themselves. As it says in the *Sublime Continuum*:

Though the nature is empty of incidental things
That have the characteristic of being separable,
It is not empty of the unsurpassable qualities
That have the characteristic of being inseparable.

Also, in the *Sutra of the Great Emptiness* it says:

Ananda, likewise when in something, something else is nonexistent, the first is empty of the second. As we correctly see what is described, the remainder that exists there, exists. Knowing what is described is correctly knowing it as it is.

Furthermore, in the *Lion's Roar of Shrimaladevi Sutra*, it says:

> Blessed One, buddha-nature is not empty of the inconceivable buddha qualities that are completely indivisible and inseparable from it, and whose number transcends that of the grains of sand in the river Ganges.

And in Manjushri's *Brief Teaching Establishing the View*, it says:

> The emptiness of analyzing the aggregates
> Is like a plantain tree that has no heart.
> The emptiness with all supreme aspects
> Is not like that.

On the basis of what is said in these scriptures and many others, proponents of zhentong proclaim that the ultimate way things are is not empty of its own essence; it is the naturally existing ultimate. This changeless ultimate is the ground of emptiness for all other things which are self-empty within it—all of the separable, relative phenomena. This is the great madhyamaka of other emptiness.

Some may object to this by saying, "Doesn't zhentong reject rangtong as established by Nagarjuna?" To this I reply that zhentong does not reject rangtong. If it is not known that the relative is empty of itself in accordance with rangtong philosophy, then it is impossible to come to the zhentong realization that the non-empty ultimate is empty of all relative phenomena other than itself.

When engaged in the analysis of relative concepts, it is true that they are found to be empty of self. However, if you were to grasp the ultimate way things are as having the same self-empty non-existence as the relative, then even by worldly standards it would be seen to be mistaken. We can only experience the nature of reality if our experience accords with what actually is. This ultimate which is empty of other must be realized through experience generated by the power of meditation.

Some say that realizing the ultimate means inferentially knowing that "the ultimate" is defined as "that which is merely not relatively true".

However, by experientially knowing such an inference there is no way of realizing the ultimate way things are. While understanding this logical ultimate that refutes the relative is indeed a necessary step along the path to experience the way things are free from the delusions of the relative, it cannot be considered the culmination of that path.

To properly distinguish the two truths, both rangtong and zhentong must be known. Actual reality is the essence of the Buddhist view and doctrine, therefore its realization must be presented in terms of experientially knowing both the non-empty ground of emptiness and the self-empty phenomena within it. To do otherwise would mean that the widely accepted thesis that "the view of the way things are is experientially realized" would be no better than saying something like "I have no idea what a vase is, but I realize that there is no water in this vase."

To illustrate this further, imagine there is a table in front of you and on that table you are supposed to perceive that there is no snake. In order to perceive "the absence of a snake on the table", you must first perceive something that you can call a "table". You must also recognize what a "snake" is. All of these concepts must be known at the same time. Only then can you determine that on the table in front of you there is no snake. This realization that "the table exists as the ground of non-existence of a snake" is the antidote by which you remove fear of a snake being there. The two truths are like that.

Like this, we can use simple worldly conventions to make emptiness easy to understand. There is no need to make it any more difficult than that. However, if one insists on extending the idea that the relative is empty of itself onto the ultimate nature, then that makes the ultimate non-existent and therefore something which cannot be realized. Such an emptiness cannot also be considered the ground of emptiness. If we hold such a view, the very notion of an ultimate becomes incomprehensible nonsense.

By definition, the experienced ground of emptiness of relative phenomena which are empty of themselves cannot itself be self-empty. The emptiness cannot simultaneously be the ground of emptiness. For if the ground of emptiness is experienced, there is nothing that can refute it. However, from the perspective of one who holds the ultimate to be self-empty, then both conventional phenomena and the ultimate would be asserted to exist as empty of themselves and ultimately non-existent. There would be no differentiation between the two. This would be like confusing animal droppings for balls of dirt.

The ultimate which is experienced cannot be empty of itself because it is the actual experience of the ultimate nature of reality. Neither experience of the incidental delusions of relative truth, nor the experience of their mere absence is equal to the experience of that actual truth. Conceptual descriptions also cannot fully describe that experience. They can only point at aspects from within the perspective of relative truth.

In Tibet, the way things are from the perspective of the deluded relative is known as *kundzop*. "Kun" means completely and "dzop" means hiding or disguising. Therefore it is that which "completely hides" the ultimate truth. In this way, kundzop is deception. This concealing, relative truth is mistaken and completely non-existent from the perspective of ultimate truth. It is definitely correct then to say that it is empty of its own essence. But if you carry that assertion over to the ultimate, the ultimate becomes a nominal state of genuine experiential realization that is neither experientially realized nor genuine. Instead, it is deprecated to being nothing at all.

When one ignores the fullness of the enlightened qualities which are realized by a zhentong view, then the view and doctrine of the Buddha are posited incompletely in terms of the mere negations of rangtong alone. This has the consequence of making both of the two truths empty of themselves. The ultimate and the relative become indistinguishable and this leads to utterly absurd and extreme conclusions. For if both of the two truths were empty falsehoods, then one could not be something false that is rejected while the other is something true that is realized. This would render the Buddhist path completely meaningless.

INTRODUCTION TO ZHENTONG

The ultimate way things are must therefore be understood as the non-empty ground that is empty of relative truth. Only then can the enlightened essence of things be correctly realized. If we do not realize that the ultimate truth can never be empty of its own essence, then even though the self-empty delusive phenomena can still be abandoned, because there is no attainment of the true phenomena of experiential fulfillment, then there is no alternative to the experience of samsara. Since the one who attains liberation is also non-existent, then there can never be a way for that being to become liberated from the extreme views of eternalism and nihilism.

The alternative to that is to completely abandon fixation onto the delusive nature of the experienced relative and then attain experience in the ultimate mode of abiding within limitless enlightened qualities. This ultimate self of the inseparable ground and result can be given the name "true self". It is the self which attains enlightenment. When we cognize that, our minds will not be deluded about all of the skilful means which liberate us from the extremes of conceptual attachment to eternalism and nihilism.

According to the proponents of rangtong though, it is not like that. If we follow their logic, then the two truths are equally deluded. There is no distinction between them. The nature of the mind and the relative are both empty of any true nature. Thus, there can be no liberation from samsaric delusion because the level of perfectly enlightened buddhahood that we strive to attain is equally delusive, nonexistent and unattainable.

In the *Sutra Benefitting Angulimala*, there is a symbolic story that represents this deluded view:

> *Once a fool saw a hailstone as a lump of precious lapis lazuli. Quickly, he hid the hailstone away in a bottle made from glass. Then, due to the heat of the midday sun, that hailstone melted. The fool squeezed the bottle to recover his treasure, but there was nothing and he became convinced that his lapis lazuli had melted into emptiness. From that moment forth,*

the man believed that he had in fact seen a real lump of lapis lazuli, but that a deluded appearance had arisen and transformed the lapis into a hailstone, which in turn melted into nothing at all. You, Manjugosha, are like that foolish person.

You also maintain that the extreme emptiness of your practice—the emptiness of nothing at all—is liberation. That extreme view of emptiness is like the example of the hailstone. Your extreme view of emptiness is conditioned by unnecessary superimpositions and is considered ignorance with respect to the liberation of a Blissful One.

In the definitive meaning, liberation has a face that is not empty. The liberation of a Blissful One is like a lump of precious lapis lazuli. Due to your ignorance that sees the two—the liberation of a Blissful One and the extreme view of emptiness—as being the same, it is like a fool maintaining that he saw a lump of lapis lazuli as a hailstone that ultimately became nothing at all.

The point of this discussion is to emphasize that no matter what a proponent of rangtong may proclaim, there is nothing that actually repudiates the zhentong view. When rangtongpas state that the ultimate experience of the way things are is self-empty, then many contradictions and incongruities arise and they are forced to patch their logic, specifically when they try to speak about the authentic nature of luminosity and innate pristine wisdom. At those times it becomes glaringly obvious that a coherent view cannot be established by joining incompatible pieces of logic.

While clearing away delusion in accordance with the realization that the relative is empty of itself is indeed the first step to liberation from samsara, in order to actually attain complete liberation we must go further until we experience with certainty the existent nature of reality described in the zhentong teachings. This is the great emptiness of other that is not empty of itself—the level of complete buddhahood which we need to attain.

This is the ultimate intention of the Victorious One, the perfect Buddha and the profound tantras which present that intention in its entirety. This includes the tantras of both the ancient translations as well as the later ones such as the Hevajra, Guhyasamaja, Mahamaya, Chakrasamvara tantras and so forth. It is especially true of the unified meaning of them all that was presented in the king of all tantras, the supremely glorious Kalachakra.

These teachings include the cherished treasures that were taught by the Victorious One himself, as well as his regent the Bodhisattva Maitreya and his followers. In particular they include the *Five Treatises of Maitreya*, the untarnished teachings of the Dharma and Kalki Kings of Shambhala, the teachings of the scholar-practitioners of the glorious Nalanda University, and the completely perfect pith instructions from the mahasiddhas of Tibet. All of these works should be read with the certainty that the good fortune of even looking at the intended meaning of the Buddha is supremely auspicious.

* * *

To benefit others, one must teach in words of conventional discourse.
Such a view must distinguish rangtong and zhentong.
By clearly knowing the nature of samsara and nirvana,
One must know what is appropriate to accept or reject.
What need is there for a doctrine that does not fulfill
these three necessities?

— *The Bodhisattva Maitreya* —
The essence of love from which the teachings of the Great Middle Way arose.

CHAPTER TWO

The Uncommon Ground, Path and Result

In accordance with the textual tradition of the Great Jonangpa, the Omniscient One possessing the Four Reliances Dolpopa Sherab Gyaltsen, I shall now teach the ultimate view of Zhentong Madhyamaka that brings forth the definitive meaning of all sutras and tantras. This is the most exalted of all views and doctrines of the snowy land of Tibet.

When determining the views of each of the Tibetan lineages, one must know how to classify their understanding of the ground, path and result. For this reason, it is very important to identify the various levels of meaning which are used to classify their associated experiences.

GROUND

The first thing that must be determined is whether the ground is an ultimate ground or merely an incidental ground. If a tradition claims that their ground is the ultimate ground, then this must be thoroughly examined. For example, if the ground is said to be an object which can be known by a conceptual consciousness, then it is by definition incidental and therefore it is not a valid basis for giving the label "ultimate ground." It is very important to examine each system in this way.

For example, if we consider the foundational consciousness in our own system of the Jonang, it is synonymous with all of the propensities for both the afflictions of samsara and the purified liberation of nirvana. Like a support in which something is deposited, it is therefore considered to be a merely incidental ground.

With regards to that which is not the ultimate ground, the Omniscient One Possessing the Four Reliances, Dolpopa Sherab Gyaltsen, stated in his *Mountain Dharma*:

> This ground of emptiness is taught as the great emptiness that is the profound way things are. Moreover, it is the ultimate emptiness of other. It is taught because it has the nature of the limitless enlightened qualities of the dharmakaya. Since it is not the emptiness which is merely established as nothing at all, this emptiness is especially exalted and for this reason is given the name "great emptiness". As it says in the sutras:
>
>> The ultimate is taught to be the pristine wisdom of the noble ones, the great emptiness, and the great nirvana. Child of noble family, what is called "great emptiness" is like this. The perfection of wisdom (the essence in which ground and result are inseparable) is known as "great emptiness".
>
> And also, it is said:
>
>> In the profound texts of secret mantra, the ultimate is called "the five unchanging aspects of great emptiness," the five syllables of great emptiness, and as glorious Vajrapani has said, "that without aspects, yet possessing all aspects." It is the cause (which is not created by other causes), the perfection of wisdom, the great emptiness endowed with all supreme aspects.
>
> And:
>
>> The great accomplishment is the great emptiness truly existing within its apprehended objects, since just that is the self-aware (primordial wisdom of) yogins.

> The exalted lord of the world, the second Kalki Pundarika, has also said in his Stainless Light commentary:
>
> *The great mind of all the buddhas is the final sixteenth phase of the vajra moon, innate pristine wisdom, the great emptiness.*
>
> And:
>
> *Likewise, the great body of all the buddhas is great emptiness.*
>
> And again:
>
> *The light of the immaculate vajra moon is the five unchanging syllables of great emptiness*
>
> In these words and so forth, [the great emptiness] is presented extensively in the Stainless Light commentary. In addition, many other completely authentic textual traditions also state that the ground of emptiness, the ultimate emptiness of other, is taught by the name "great emptiness." We should be knowledgeable of how a great many of these traditions have just this as their intended meaning.

With these words and so forth, Dolpopa taught the uncommon ground that is especially exalted surpassing the ordinary. As is said there, the nondual nature of the dharmadhatu and primordial wisdom is the ground of the emptiness of relative delusive appearances. There, in the midst of incidental defilements, all defiled beings abide in a defiled manner. The suchness of that is the uncommon ground—buddha-nature.

Moreover, in the *General Commentary on the Teaching*, the Omniscient One Possessing the Four Reliances taught:

> *The ultimate ground of being together with defilements is like that.*

In addition, in both the root text and the commentary on the *Sublime Continuum* which were written by the most excellent of all the buddha's children, the regent of the Victorious One the Bodhisattva Maitreya, it says:

> *Afflicted states of mind are like being buried deep in the earth,*
> *While the nature of the Tathagata is like a precious treasure. As it says:*
>
> > *As in the house of a poor man, under the earth,*
> > *An inexhaustible treasure might exist,*
> > *But the man did not know that, and that treasure too*
> > *Would not say to him, "I am here."*
> > *likewise, the precious treasure that is concealed within the mind*
> > *Is the nature of phenomena resting undefiled, with nothing that*
> > *needs to be cleared away.*
> > *By not realizing it, the poor man's sufferings,*
> > *Many and continuous, are experienced by all beings.*
>
> As in the poor man's house, a precious treasure is concealed, but it is not said that the man is the owner of a precious treasure because the man does not know about it. Sentient beings are like that poor man with respect to the dharma treasure that abides in the house of their mind. So that it may be attained by them, completely pure sages take birth.

When it is taught that the ground is defiled, that apparent defilement is only from the perspective of sentient beings who have the continuum of the ground as their essence. Needless to say, even though it is taught as defiled, the ground itself is primordially free of adventitious stains.

PATH

The stages to complete realization of this uncommon ground are the hidden meaning of both the first and second turnings. However, in the uncommon path of Kalachakra, through the six branched yoga of the completion stage—the path of the definitive meaning of the tantras—the great bliss of the unchanging dharmadhatu is worked with directly.

It is established by the experience of the former great sages who have practiced these six yogas. Through this supreme profound path, the vivid presence of luminosity—the primordial bodies of a Buddha—are attained by even ordinary people. Also, in the pure realm of Shambhala, the result of buddhahood can even be attained in as little as a single year. Furthermore, even in this impure world, the union of these bodies can be established in one human lifetime. As Dolpopa taught in the *General Commentary on the Teaching*:

The final part of the path is the six branched yoga.

RESULT

Again, in the glorious *Kalachakra Tantra*, it says:

As for what it bestows, it completely bestows the result of buddhahood.

This teaches the uncommon result of the victorious tradition of the Jonang. Then, as the victorious Maitreya said in his *Sublime Continuum*:

As it was before, so it is later,
The unchanging nature of phenomena.

Here, even though the ground and result are inseparable in reality, from the temporary perspective of a sentient being the ground appears as defiled. Such a being establishes the mere convention that they are separate.

The result of buddhahood manifests when individual people rely upon the oral instructions of a qualified master and practice the extraordinarily profound path of the six branched yoga. Through this process, they gradually exhaust the assembly of discursive conceptual thoughts within their continuums, as well as all of the defilements that constitute the two obscurations of the ultimate dharmakaya—the primordial, great and supreme nature itself.

Not newly established in the result and manifesting like the ever-present sun free from enveloping clouds, buddha-nature abides eternally within sentient beings. Through the naturally clear, innate radiance of suchness, our own distinctive qualities are completely manifest. And yet, from the perspective of the individual beings themselves, the perception of their being newly transformed into undefiled suchness is given the name "attaining the result." As the Omniscient One taught in the *General Commentary on the Teaching*:

The ultimate result of separation, the result, is like that.

There the unsurpassable result of separation that has the nature of the four bodies and five primordial wisdoms is briefly explained to be the result in this extraordinary tradition.

* * *

A ground that is not eternally stable is not a refuge.
A path that has no pristine wisdom cannot liberate.
A result that ripens through development is not eternal.
May the inseparable cause and effect of buddha-nature be victorious.

CHAPTER THREE

The Seven Kinds of Misconception

When analyzing the misconceptions and modes of non-realization, there are seven misconceptions in relation to: (1) how ultimate reality is truly existent; (2) how the nature of suchness does not arise interdependently; (3) how suchness is a true self; (4) how the relative does not appear to the buddhas; (5) how the suchness of buddha-nature transcends the realm of words and concepts; (6) how the relative has never existed; and (7) how there are no faults if one establishes suchness as independent.

1. HOW ULTIMATE REALITY IS TRULY EXISTENT

Many learned scholars in Tibet say that the inseparable ground and result asserted by the Jonang is buddha-nature, and that the ultimate way things are is the truth which is found by the primordial wisdom of a noble one's meditative absorption. While they agree that this is the ultimate nature, they say that while it is true, it does not truly exist. The reasoning for saying that it does not truly exist is as follows.

They say that something which truly exists cannot arise interdependently and vice versa. Furthermore, they say that all existent phenomena arise interdependently. To prove this statement, they rely on the reasonings of the arising and ceasing of the four extremes and the arising and ceasing of the four limits.

Taking an apple as an example, they say that an apple that exists conventionally is determined through reasoning to not exist inherently as an apple. This is similar to saying "the apple exists but does not exist."

From the perspective of how ordinary people speak, that is a contradictory statement.

While many such reasonings have been put forward by dogmatic logicians, an apple that is apprehended and pointed out with the finger exists as an apple. That apple is established by the experience of an apple. All of the forms, sounds, smells, tastes, tangible qualities and so forth that are the characteristics of an apple exist in that moment, therefore, since each one's essence is established by perception. It then follows that in this situation, we can say the apple exists as an apple.

This conclusion is universally accepted in accordance with how we speak. If valid cognition establishes that this or that phenomena are there, then this or that phenomena must conventionally be there. It is not a valid response to say that they are not truly there in a special philosophical sense.

Moreover, when this or that are perceived conventionally, then the essence of this or that which are the criteria for perceiving them must also exist conventionally. This can be known from the direct meaning of the words. For example, if earth is perceived, then it must exist as earth. If water is perceived, then it must exist as water and so forth. This is certainly true. Likewise, if we say that something is the ultimate, then it has to exist as the ultimate. If we say that it is relative, then it has to exist as the relative and so forth. This is the ordinary way in which language works.

In accordance with genuine reasoning, that which is true and that which is truly existent are not distinguished as different. This is clearly taught in the sutras and treatises such as in the *Lankavatara Sutra*, where it teaches on truth by saying:

> *Mahamati, the nature of phenomena that I and these Tathagatas have comprehended, the existence of phenomena, the unchanging nature of phenomena, their suchness, their authenticity and truth; these exist.*

Similarly, in Nagarjuna's *Root Verses on the Middle Way*, he says:

> *Nirvana, the single truth.*

Also, in his *Essence of Zhentong Madhyamaka*, Jetsun Taranatha writes:

> *Because the non-delusive primordial wisdom of the noble ones is experienced, it is established as true. Since it is unchanging, it is eternally stable and permanent. Buddha-nature, that which abides along with the excellent qualities such as the major and minor marks and so forth, is taught by many synonyms in all the tantras of secret mantra.*

Then in the *Distinction of the Two Modes*, he says:

> *Since the ultimate dharmadhatu is truly existent, while it is not empty of itself, it is emptiness nonetheless. This is because it is empty of all proliferating elaborations such as grasper, grasped and so forth which are other than itself.*

In his *Root of the Middle Way of the Great Vehicle*, Taranatha speaks about buddha-nature by saying:

> *Truly established by the primordial wisdom of the victorious ones,*
> *Since it is an object which is known, realized, seen and experienced,*
> *It is within the scope of a discriminating, self-aware primordial wisdom.*

Also, in the *Wish Fulfilling Gem of the Middle Way*, he says:

> *By recognising that it is free from conceptual elaborations, it is truly existent.*

In these passages, that which is said to be true is also truly existent. Furthermore, if it were possible for a vase to not have an established essence of a vase, or for gold to not have the essence of gold, then statements about vases and gold could not be verified. It would be impossible to come to conclusions through reasoning. Moreover, denying the existence of what exists does not yield conventionally meaningful statements. Such reasonings which only play with literal words have a mere semblance of reasoning.

For them, while the extreme of proliferating conceptual labels is indeed non-existent, by these tenets becoming an obstruction to hearing about and contemplating the natural state, the resultant benefit and happiness will be very small indeed. In the end, there can be no genuine focus for such objects of reasoning.

* * *

> *Without true existence, the way things are is contradiction.*
> *The self-emptiness of the nature of dharmas is contradiction.*
> *Presenting doctrines without assertions is contradiction.*
> *Transcending paths that have contradictions is important.*

2. HOW THE NATURE OF SUCHNESS DOES NOT ARISE INTERDEPENDENTLY

In the *Root Verses on the Middle Way*, the glorious protector, Arya Nagarjuna teaches:

> *Except for arising interdependently,*
> *No phenomenon exists.*
> *Likewise, no phenomenon exists*
> *That is not emptiness.*

In this point, it is understood within the Jonang Tradition, that the idea of "no phenomena exist that are not dependent on some other phenomena" means that all relative phenomena arise interdependently. However, the opposite is true for the ultimate nature of phenomena.

Some might think, "Well, if such a ground exists, it will indeed be pervasive, but though you say it is emptiness, its mode of abiding is not like that of emptiness." Responding to this, the exalted one Maitreya taught:

> *Nonexistent emptiness is known,*
> *And likewise there is existent emptiness.*
> *As well as emptiness that is the nature. If these are known,*
> *That is called "knowledge of emptiness."*

THE SEVEN MISCONCEPTIONS

— *The Bodhisattva Manjushri* —
The living embodiment of primordial wisdom.

He goes on to say:

> *There is the nonexistent emptiness of the imputed,*
> *The existent nature of the dependent,*
> *And the thoroughly established,*
> *Ultimate great emptiness of the other.*

This is how emptiness should be explained in accordance with the Jonang tradition.

Furthermore, nothing which arises interdependently can be said to have the same kind of emptiness as the ultimate nature of reality. Everything which arises interdependently is necessarily empty of itself. In such an emptiness where something is "empty of itself," the meaning of "empty" is that some knowable object itself is non-existent. There is no other meaning than just this. Rather than there being any sort of additional understanding beyond this, all other ways of understanding "emptiness of itself" are just collections of conceptually superimposed imputations.

Interdependent arising should be understood as follows: (1) the mutual causes and conditions of phenomena and (2) the interdependent establishment of phenomena arising from mutual dependence which is therefore labelled as "interdependent". Such interdependent things are empty of themselves and therefore non-existent. There is no other way to understand this.

On the other hand, if a logical syllogism is presented where the subject, the ultimate way things are—buddha-nature—is incompatible with interdependent arising, then one would reply as follows. If buddha-nature were to arise interdependently, it would exist as an other-dependent nature and therefore would lack independence. If that were the case, then buddha-nature would not transcend impermanence and suffering. The ultimate state to be strived for and attained would not transcend impermanence and suffering. If that were true, then the ultimate which is attained by those who strive for liberation would be unsuitable to call

THE SEVEN MISCONCEPTIONS

"liberation." Moreover, even though it is said "the ultimate is the union of emptiness and dependent arising," there would be no way to unify the two within the natural state, for that which is "empty" means it is non-existent.

As long as you agree with dependent arising, then you must agree that it is real. Something cannot be both real and unreal. Otherwise you would have to say that real and unreal are not contradictory in order to ensure that the union of emptiness and dependent arising could exist. For this reason, if you agree that the real and the unreal are non-contradictory and also that the functional and the non-functional are non-contradictory, then you are contradicting your own doctrine and also contradicting logic even more.

Furthermore if one makes such a statement, it will certainly not make sense from the perspective of ordinary people in this world since it will directly contradict their wordly conventions. It would also contradict the teaching that the buddhas do not dispute the worldly "I". When it is explained like that, it should be known that self-emptiness and interdependent arising cannot be explained in any other way than as being two.

For centuries, logicians have been claiming that all phenomena are self-empty and dependently arisen. However, at this time, those statements are taken to be supreme over everything and most of the time they are just accepted without actually analysing them. If someone were to analyse them, then people who said such things would be few and far between. It would not even be hard to imagine that they might even become non-existent. As the lord of the learned ones Gendun Chöphel has said:

All ancient ones proclaimed the tradition of the view.
All modern ones' thoughts are the illusions of mara.
The kingdom of Dharma is the tradition of Tibet.

These words point to an important reality regarding the natural disposition in people that is worth thinking about.

The opposite of the above statements about there being a union of dependent arising and emptiness is the teaching that in the ultimate way things are, buddha-nature is the dharmakaya in which ground and fruition are inseparable. If one can reach that understanding, then buddha-nature is transcendent, going beyond the mere dependent arising of material causes and conditions. Untouched by the thousands of refutations of a logician's reasoning, we can reach confidence in the topics of the vast and profound and also become accustomed to this truth by meditating on it.

The view which is rooted in non-conceptual primordial wisdom is vast and carefree. Experience and realization flow out of gaining familiarity with joining one's own continuum with the ultimate expanse. When this is done, it will certainly bring the full measure of the results and the accomplishment of our ultimate aims. The way things are—buddha-nature—is established by yogic perception to be the eternally stable, unchanging nature.

Since that is certain, buddha-nature necessarily transcends dependent arising. If you understand this way of thinking, then those who have only slightly studied the textual tradition are left shocked and without recourse, citing these words of the learned forefather Nagarjuna:

> *Except for arising interdependently,*
> *No phenomenon exists.*
> *Likewise, no phenomenon exists*
> *That is not emptiness.*

As has been explained previously, the scope of this statement should be restricted to relative phenomena. However, due to its meaning being so clear, this passage is very important and therefore worth looking into again. When it says, "Except for arising interdependently, no phenomena exist," the referent of the statement is *phenomena* (Skt. dharma). It does not include even one part of *the nature of phenomena* (Skt. dharmata). The nature of phenomena—buddha-nature—cannot be understood as the subject here. Therefore it should be easy to see that Nagarjuna is not teaching that the nature of phenomena is dependent arising.

Moreover, while the Jonang accept that the six logical works of Nagarjuna are valid commentaries on the intention of the middle turning, the absolute nature of phenomena—buddha-nature—is not considered to be their main focus. Therefore these works do not discredit buddha-nature, for as Nagarjuna himself has declared:

The sutras teaching emptiness,
As many as were taught by the Victorious One;
By all these the afflictions are reversed,
But the nature is not impaired.

What this says is that all of the teachings on emptiness that were taught by the Victorious One were for the purpose of reversing the afflictions. They refute the afflictions which are rooted in the self-grasping of the two forms of self—the self of persons and the self of phenomena. However, the ground of emptiness—buddha-nature—is never refuted nor disparaged. These same scriptures very clearly teach that buddha-nature—the expanse of reality or the ultimate truth itself—is not empty of its own essence.

In order to teach that the ultimate way things are—the ultimate truth—is not a mere vacuous emptiness, the great sage the blessed Buddha taught in the *Sutra Teaching the Absence of Decrease and Increase*:

Shariputra, the ultimate should be realized with faith.
Shariputra, "the ultimate" is a verbal expression for the nature of sentient beings.
Shariputra, "buddha-nature" is a verbal expression for the Dharmakaya.

Some may then ask, "Isn't the intended meaning of those terms merely the kind of emptiness where all phenomena are simply not established at all and are the causal propensities of buddhahood?" I would say no, because what is being taught is the immeasurable pristine wisdom of buddhahood—that which possesses limitless buddha qualities.

To say that the ultimate is the mere non-establishment of phenomena and that buddha-nature is the mere propensity for buddhahood is not established in any way by scriptures or reasoning. Therefore, to insist that these statements are true serves no practical purpose. If such people continue to insist in this way, for their sake we will need to make prayers that they stop.

* * *

If there is a nature of phenomena, it is buddha-nature.
If there is great bliss, it is contradictory to say it is interdependent.
It is contradictory to say the self-empty are ultimate.
It is contradictory to say the dependent are ultimate.

3. HOW SUCHNESS IS A TRUE SELF

From among the many learned ones in the land of snow, there are many who are arrogant about their learning. Their minds are so full that they have very little room to even consider different ways of thinking. As soon as they even hear words which don't fit within their own limited preconceptions, they become disgusted. Such people can only be seen as objects of compassion.

Regardless of what others may think, the Jonangpas refer to the ultimate way things are—buddha-nature—to be the ultimate or true self. That is seen to be the intended meaning of the Buddha from Dolpo. In the irreversible teaching of the Age of Perfection, it is said "that which does not establish habitual propensities is the self."

If someone were to confuse this assertion as maintaining that the well-known objects of refutation—the self of persons and the self of phenomena—should not be refuted, then that is astonishingly and incredibly incoherent. This is what we refer to as "the incurable view".

Such a view implies that there cannot be genuine contemplation or meditation in accordance with the Ten Sutras of Definitive Meaning and so forth that are found in the Buddha's final turning of the Wheel of Dharma, nor in the authentic commentaries on those teachings. However, when meditating on the way things are in accordance with these scriptures, it is possible to have clear signs of reaching uninterrupted experience. This state is referred to by the glorious and victorious Jonangpa as "selfhood." Again and again in the Ten Sutras of Definitive Meaning, and elsewhere, this sign is distinguished by nothing other than the word "self."

This ultimate self is not even remotely similar to the two kinds of self which are known by all as objects of refutation and which are generally found in the texts on madhyamaka and valid cognition. This ultimate self is called "buddha-nature" and "the ultimate way things are." These same terms are commonly used in Tibet to refer to the ultimate ground. That ground is referred to in these sutras not only by the conventional designation of "self", but also as "the great self," "the true self," "the absolute self" and so forth, due to the many distinctive qualities that it possesses.

This shows that these terms originated only from the words of the Victorious One and from the authentic commentaries on their meaning which were written by the noble scholar-practitioners of India and Tibet. They were in no way terms which were invented by the Jonang. As it says in the *Mahaparinirvana Sutra* that was translated by Devachandra:

> "Self" here has the meaning of buddha-nature. Though indeed this nature of the buddha exists within all sentient beings, it is obscured by afflicted phenomena so that sentient beings cannot see their selfhood as it is.

Also, the glorious *Tantra of the Unsullied* states:

> The collective self of all buddhas
> Will quickly grant its blessings.
> The collective self of all buddhas
> Is the self of all buddhas combined.

Again, in the *Great Nirvana Sutra* it says:

> Buddha-nature is not completely selfless. What kind of phenomena is the self? It is true, genuine, eternal, existent, sovereign, unchanging and indestructible. Just that should be called "self." Thus a great physician is knowledgeable about medicinal milk.

Here "milk" is a metaphor for buddha-nature. Through this analogy he is saying that even though a particular kind of milk may be an excellent medicine for beings to be tamed, some physicians may not know how to use this medicine. This may be the result of being unskilled in the use of medicines in general or perhaps due to being wrongly opposed to using this milk as a medicine.

Similarly, for those attached to a conventional self, that self is refuted in the middle turning of the Dharma. For those who are able to understand selflessness like that, the existence of an absolute self which is the inseparability of ground and result is taught as "milk" in the *Great Nirvana Sutra* and so forth of the final turning. As it says:

> *The unconditioned is great nirvana, that which transcends impermanence. Permanence is the self. That self is complete purity. That which is completely pure is called "bliss." Permanence, bliss, self and complete purity are the Tathagata.*

With regards to what was taught there, the Omniscient One—the Great Jonangpa Possessing the Four Reliances, the Buddha from Dolpo—gathered together many passages from the ocean-like sutras and tantras and having developed clarity in their meaning, he explained them.

* * *

The non-existent, deluded self is totally absent.
However, the supreme self is ultimate buddhahood.
If the ultimate way things are is not a self,
Who then abandons the obscurations and attains the accumulations?

4. HOW THE RELATIVE DOES NOT APPEAR TO THE BUDDHAS

Even though the relative does not appear to the buddhas, they never have the fault of not knowing it. This is due to the fact that the intention of the

Victorious One and his regent is that even though the deluded appearances of the relative do not arise, the suchness of the relative is known just as it is.

It is taught in this way because all conventional phenomena arise for sentient beings who are deluded about the way objects appear. If those same phenomena were to appear to the buddhas, then it would be like you were saying that the buddhas are deluded.

Additionally, that which is real in the relative, like water for example, appears in many different ways not only for the buddhas but for sentient beings as well. As it says in Asanga's *Compendium of the Great Vehicle*:

Due to minds of a single thing being different,
They are asserted to not be established as the ultimate.

Like it is said there, for every single thing there exists many different appearances in accordance with the minds of beings. Moreover, since that which appears to the buddha are supposed to be absolutely true—since thinking otherwise would be a direct contradiction to the meaning of Asanga's *Compendium of the Great Vehicle*, and especially since the buddha's pristine wisdom is the primordial wisdom which exhausts the two obscurations—they cannot be the approximate cause for relative appearances.

Due to relative appearances having no connection with the immeasurable appearances of the ultimate, they are mutually exclusive. When there are ultimate appearances, relative appearances never arise. With regards to this, Maitreya says in his *Distinguishing Phenomena and the Nature of Phenomena*:

When that appears, the nature of phenomena does not appear,
And when that does not appear, the nature of phenomena appears.

Thus it is clearly taught that the relative does not appear to the buddhas. This is the intention of all the authentic Victorious Ones and their children.

Even though the relative does not appear to the buddhas, the nature of realization is implicitly known. If the buddhas know how the relative is even though it does not appear, that does not contradict correct scripture and reasoning.

* * *

Relative appearances appear only as delusion.
Since the perfect buddhas have forever exhausted delusion,
They know all relative phenomena, but have no false appearance.
This is not known by fools, but is known by the competent.

5. HOW THE SUCHNESS OF BUDDHA-NATURE TRANSCENDS THE REALM OF WORDS AND CONCEPTS

The ultimate truth which transcends concepts appears only to the undeluded. It is the ultimate way things are. Relative truth consists of only deluded appearances and for this reason, the two truths must always be different.

Furthermore, when something within the realm of words or concepts is grasped, it must be labelled as a phenomena that is classified by specific expressions of meaning. Such things are definitely within the realm of the conceptual intellect. Regarding this, the Blessed Victorious One taught in the *Lankavatara Sutra*:

The vehicle of individual self-awareness is not the realm of logicians.

This idea is also taught in Jetsun Taranatha's *Wish Fulfilling Gem of the Middle Way*, where it says:

If it is realized by concepts, it is a mundane elaboration.

As it says there, whatever is grasped as a conceptual object is a deluded elaboration. Since such elaborations are necessarily inferior and provisional, they are never permissible as ultimate truth. However, refuting such words out of context (as many people tend to do) is like saying that the referents of words such as "buddha-nature" must be conceptual when in actuality they refer to non-conceptual objects. This idea is completely rejected within the pure presentation of our own system. Regardless of what other traditions may say, it is very important that we maintain the complete purity of our own stainless tradition.

The reason for this is that the individual forefathers of our tradition, many hundreds of years ago, grasped the essence of the teachings through faith, exertion, meditative concentration and so forth, just like the essence of butter arises by churning milk. To produce distorted personal fabrications that contaminate that essence for the sole purpose of saving face in the eyes of others is extremely confused behaviour. Is this not clear?

Some individuals whose understanding is not extensive and whose mind lacks depth fear that their mental endeavours cannot move forward if the ultimate is not within the realm of words and concepts. They are extremely concerned about whether they will be able to propagate their own view and defend it against objections. This is due only to such persons of limited understanding thinking that we humans have no other method for resolving the way things are if not by words and concepts.

Therefore they think that whatever is done by those practicing hearing, contemplation and meditation for the sake of realizing the non-conceptual way things are in accordance with the third turning must be practicing in vain. Since the blissful way things are is said to transcend words and concepts in reliance on the teachings of all the sutras of the final turning as well as all of the tantras of secret mantra, they believe that such reality cannot manifest in one's experience.

Due to the desire to further their own personal endeavours and also their attachment to literal words taken out of context and so forth, such people exchange devious words about alleged consequences. By putting forward many apparent lines of reasoning, both the challenger and defender in such a debate are just wasting their own and others' time. They are wasting this precious human body with its freedoms and endowments which is more rare and precious than even gold. Other than this, such debates have no purpose nor value at all.

To understand why this is the case, when someone says that "the ultimate is not the object of words and conceptions," they mean that the ultimate way things are—buddha-nature—is endowed with all possible aspects as its expression. Saying that has no fault of contradiction nor incongruity.

However, since postulates about the "ultimate way things are" must be presented through relative words and concepts, they are necessarily analyzed by a mind which is deluded by the meaning of abstract conceptions. Within this scope something being endowed with all possible aspects as its expression is impossible. Nevertheless, the ultimate way things are is not within the scope of words and concepts aside from being explained by words which are. In the individual speculations about the purpose and power of making such statements, individual minds conclude that the ultimate must be non-existent. It is important to realize that such a conclusion is completely unfounded.

Needlessly spending time on an unnecessary mental exercise where the imagined necessity is entirely pointless is just quarreling without necessity. Expending one's energy on a level where one's energy need not be spent is simply wrong conduct and a waste of our precious freedoms and endowments. It is important to know that entrusting the innermost reality of the mind to the ever shifting movements of discursive thoughts is only foolishness.

* * *

In the mere words and concepts of the deceptive relative,
Only the relative's own objects can exist.
However, when the ultimate way things are is being taught,
How could there be faults or errors in focusing on the innermost mind?

6. HOW THE RELATIVE HAS NEVER EXISTED

When explaining the ways in which the relative does and does not exist, in general one should always focus the mind on the two truths as appropriate. There is no third way of explaining that does not rely on the two truths.

In particular though, at the time of actually grasping the objects of negation in this tradition of tenets, after reflecting on the ground of negation—emptiness or the ultimate truth—what is refuted is said to be non-existent in the ground. Similarly, relative existence and non-existence can be explained after reflecting on the final mode of abiding. When that is not done, the final mode of abiding is necessarily not final and ultimate truth is necessarily not ultimate truth.

Why is this so? In the Jonang system, relative phenomena are necessarily non-existent because "the relative" are equivalent to "deluded appearances." Thus everything which is classified as a deluded appearance is relative. As those deluded appearances are exhausted within an individual's mind, the essence of the mind of the knower becomes more and more manifest. Finally, the mind of the relative is completely exhausted, leaving only the ultimate.

That mind of the undefiled ultimate is the ground of emptiness—buddha-nature. When purified, the mind transforms into the complete non-appearance of the relative. Even though there are causes for the appearance of relative phenomena, there is never non-appearance. Due to not having the causes for appearing, there is non-appearance. Just this was taught by Taranatha.

Specifically, when identifying the objects of negation for both self-emptiness and other-emptiness, in the *Elegant Explanation of the Heart Sutra that was Never Known Before*, Taranatha taught:

> *All phenomena of sight and sound are primordially unestablished. Therefore, space is pervaded by changless primordial wisdom, free from all elaborations. The completely perfect and completely pure meaning of the selflessness of phenomena is the sublime.*

As it says here, all of the apparent phenomena of sights and sounds are taught as not being primordially established. While they are true relatively, they are non-existent in the ultimate. We should not attempt to avoid the criticism of others who are attached to mere words by rejecting our own tradition and saying that they need not be non-existent there.

Rather we should respond by saying that our own textual tradition is also non-existent in the ultimate. Because that is so, our tradition fulfills the function of non-existence. Anyone who says that is not so wanders far from the four reliances. As Taranatha taught in the *Ornament of Zhentong Madhyamaka*:

> *Due to existing in the relative, it is said to be existent.*
> *Nevertheless, not existing in the relative, it is said to be non-existent.*
> *Even though not existing in the ultimate, it is said to be existent.*
> *Not relying on the ultimate, one relies on the conventional.*
>
> *When consciousness actually exists, it is said to be existent.*
> *When consciousness actually doesn't exist, it fulfills the function of being non-existent.*
> *Even though primordial wisdom doesn't actually appear, it is said "to exist."*
> *After abandoning primordial wisdom, one relies on the mind alone.*
>
> *In the Dharma which was taught by the Conqueror, this is mostly false.*
> *All genuine commentaries are said to be truth.*
> *However, if the root is false then the commentaries can not possibly be true.*
> *Their Dharma is abandoned and one relies on individuals.*
>
> *Understanding reality through the two kinds of negation,*
> *Logicians and those like them put their reliance on words.*
> *Those who mostly give rise to the consequences of self-emptiness*
> *Have wandered far from the four reliances.*

What is taught there and so forth is very well established.

* * *

Even though the relative was never there, eat the food and enjoy!
With the pure discipline that abandons negativity and clinging to virtue,
There is no need to weary ourselves, since they surely have no fruition.
Illusory beings also bestow joy and inspiration.

7. HOW THERE ARE NO FAULTS IF ONE ESTABLISHES SUCHNESS AS INDEPENDENT

Previously I spoke of the way that the Jonang maintain that the ultimate way things are is independently established. Later in this book I will be presenting various proofs for clearing away the faults of thinking this is a view similar to theistic non-buddhists or that this view is completely unrelated to Buddhist scripture and reasoning. Since these are rather technical discussions, I have placed them later so that you can gradually develop your interest in these subtle forms of analysis.

However, in brief, I would like to address here that some people, even now, note that the Jonangpas say that the nature of phenomena is "independently established". Therefore they insist that the Jonang are outside Buddhism and that the Jonang are in some way trying to conceal their heretical nature. This is a false accusation and it is important to eliminate such disingenuous criticism. These biased traditions of making two sides are merely substituting thought for nonsense. Other than that, there does not appear to be any great goal or purpose for doing this.

The truth is that the exact phrase "establishment is independent" is not found in the Jonang textual tradition. However, there is no point in debating this idea. If such things are said, the same argument may well be said for all the important key terms used within the textual traditions of all Tibetan lineages.

If one searches for complete phrases that exist or do not exist in the sutras and tantras, how could one ever find them all? For example, in the tradition of Ganden Monastery it is said that the words "what is to be refuted is inherent existence" are very important and yet this complete phrase seems not to be found in any sutras or tantras. Likewise if all the words that are grasped as important within the various Tibetan lineages must be found in the sutras and tantras just as they are, then it seems to be an impossible requirement.

Though the words "establishment is independent" are not found in the sutras and tantras, saying that the Jonang view is no better than the impermanence of the external world is simply nonsense. According to the view of the Age of Perfection, the Zhentong Madhyamaka of the Omniscient One Possessing the Four Reliances—Dolpopa Sherab Gyaltsen—there are a great many scriptural sources that explain how the nature of phenomena is "established." Similarly, there are also a great many scriptures and reasonings for why the nature of phenomena is independent, as has been compiled within the scriptural traditions of the sutras and tantras. These truths are exceedingly evident and clear, and since they arise over and over again, they are made increasingly certain.

If we explain just a little bit of how the nature of phenomena is independently established to those who have never heard this approach before, then it is like this. When such a nature is established, it is seen to be both real and eternal. How could such a nature of phenomena ever be established as something unreal? This approach avoids digging oneself into a nihilistic pit by thinking that an independent nature of phenomena is impossible.

When all of one's doubts are cleared away, then the nature of phenomena is said to be established. This is because the ultimate way things are must necessarily not be empty of itself, while it definitely must be empty of other. If that nature cannot be empty of its own essence and must be empty of anything other than itself, then it is said to be "established."

Not being an aspect which is cut off through elimination, it exists as all of the countless enlightened qualities. Buddha-nature is therefore endowed with all aspects. Without the faults of contradiction or incongruity, buddha-nature is proven to be eternal. Because it is eternal, it cannot be considered a relative entity. If buddha-nature were a relative entity, it could not have the capacity to manifest all enlightened qualities, be endowed with all supreme qualities and so forth.

For all these reasons, the ultimate way things are—buddha-nature—is established as transcending the duality of relative entities and non-entities. As such, the nature of phenomena is necessarily independently established. This ultimate way things are transcends relative phenomena which are found empty through non-affirming negation.

Entities which are established through imputation are excluded from being established as independent phenomena. Buddha-nature must be the ultimate truth or the ultimate way things are. If it is not independent, then it must be other-dependent, which means that it is a dependent arising. That would mean that buddha-nature is impermanent, which means that it must be suffering. All such absurd consequences would arise. Therefore buddha-nature could not be the nature of phenomena. Through non-affirming negation, it would be found to be unreal.

Finally it would follow that it is necessarily non-existent because it is necessarily empty of itself. This is because, "empty of itself" and "nonexistent" are equivalent. This is common knowledge. In particular, what is not other-empty must be self-empty and therefore non-existent. This means that if the way things are is self-empty, then the ultimate natural state of all phenomena must be nothing at all.

For this reason I suggest that for all exponents of doctrine, whoever they may be, rather than holding a view of non-affirming negation that entails nothingness, it would be better to maintain that the ultimate is free from conceptual elaborations. To say it is "free from all assertions" is also suitable.

In brief, if one maintains that the ultimate way things are is empty of its own essence, then this is no different than maintaining that it is a non-affirming negation. That is the same as saying that the nature of phenomena is non-existent. If you do that, then there is only one solitary relative truth. Limitless faults would then follow from this foolish statement.

Therefore the ultimate truth—the great emptiness that is empty of other—is necessarily established as real. If it is not, the ultimate would be non-existent. The ground of emptiness would be non-existent. The ground of purification of the obscurations would be non-existent. These are just a few of the many other irreversible faults that would occur.

Through this and other especially great teachings of the Age of Perfection, as well as the subsequent Age of Three Parts and so forth, the nature of phenomena is proclaimed as established and independent. Between the two options of the nature of phenomena being either negated or affirmed, it is definitely affirmed. With regard to how this definite affirmation must be established as a real phenomena, in *Differentiating the View*, the Omniscient One Dolpopa taught:

> *The non-empty ultimate is itself established.*
> *Thus it exists without deception as truth.*
> *That existence is primordial existence.*
> *It is established as the intrinsic nature.*
>
> *Negation is established by refutation.*
> *Establishment is negated by refutation.*
> *The established is the way things really are.*
> *Such is the tradition of the competent.*

Also, as he says in the *Mountain Dharma*:

> *In regard to that, because the nature does not arise from causes and conditions and is unfabricated, (because it is independently naturally arisen) it is taught that it is not dependent on anything other than itself.*

So once established, it cannot be established as a relative entity. This is echoed by Taranatha in his *Supremely Clear Appearance of Union*:

> *According to wordly opinion, if it is certain that in a cave there is a lion, it can be realized that a fox will not be found there or if it is certain that the sun has arisen, it can be realized that darkness does not exist. Similarly, if it is certain that the ultimate primordial wisdom has primordially existed in all of the three realms, then it can be realized that the three realms of a relative conceptual consciousness have never primordially existed.*

> *Therefore by meditating on bliss and empty-form, fixation to relative entities and their appearing as real things are both reversed. This union of empty-form and immutable bliss transcends the extremes of entities and non-entities, existence and non-existence, what "is" and "is not." Therefore, it is the uncompounded ultimate.*

> *The establishment of relative entities are never independent.*
> *However, without reasoning, one takes them for real entities.*

> *These words are saying that if one insistently imposes such a view, many absurd consequences will be experienced. Freedom from extremes in your tradition certainly imposes real things and non-existence. However, what point is there responding to this, since without reasoning you are doing the same thing?*

If one were to say that the textual tradition in which these words are set forth is generally not a Buddhist view and that it is certainly the language of theistic non-buddhists, then I would reply that if one thinks that the way things are and truth are always non-existent, then holding fast to this sort of of coarse conceptual labelling which should be abandoned is simply an inferior way of grasping the supreme view.

* * *

Since it is the way things are, it is not the mere absence of negation.
That which is established without contradiction or incongruity
is the supreme expanse.
That which is established as eternally stable is independent.
Because it is independent, it is not dependent on others.

CHAPTER FOUR

The Eighteen Unique Qualities of the Jonang View

The Jonang view can best be explained by way of eighteen unique qualities: (1) being uncommon; (2) having great confidence; (3) being profound and firm; (4) being harmonious; (5) being completely free; (6) possessing the profound meaning; (7) being incontrovertible; (8) having strength; (9) being pure; (10) having clarity; (11) being undeluded; (12) penetrating to the deepest meaning; (13) being unmistaken; (14) being rooted in practice; (15) having an intimate approach; (16) being experiential; (17) having unity; and (18) being incomparable.

1. THE UNIQUE QUALITY OF BEING UNCOMMON DUE TO ITS COMPETENCE IN DISTINGUISHING BETWEEN COMPLETE AND INCOMPLETE DHARMAS

In the teachings of the Tibetan lineages, there are generally four well-known ages—the age of perfection, the age of three parts, the age of two parts and the age of strife. There are two ways to consider these ages: (1) as the good and bad times which arise successively due to the shared karma of sentient beings, and (2) as the quality of the dharma at the times of training in the sacred teachings. Here, however, they are also measured in relation to the mere meaning of that Dharma.

The unrivalled Omniscient One Possessing the Four Reliances made many great distinctions. These distinctions include distinguishing the truth, distinguishing the real and the unreal, distinguishing the permanent and the impermanent, distinguishing the ultimate and the relative and so forth. When we speak about these distinctions from the perspective of the view, if the presentation by way of the unique characteristics that distinguishes the view is to be explained a little, it can be distinguished in terms of the degree of ignorance and delusion that does not enter into the ultimate mode of abiding which is finally realized.

With regards to this, the master Padmasambhava has said:

Time is unchanging. Humans change.

There he teaches that there is no reason to blame time for it is the perspective of human beings who change. Similarly, bursting forth from the exalted mind of great primordial wisdom, the view of the Omniscient One Possessing the Four Reliances, the Buddha from Dolpo, is the way of identifying the Dharma of the Age of Perfection. After this, there are the stages of having three parts, having two parts and then degeneration. This is the extraordinary method for classifying the view.

What the view is like in these ages is related to the intention of the three turnings of the wheels of the completely victorious Buddha, as well as the explanations of his regent Maitreya and the commentaries of the Dharma and Kalkis Kings of Shambhala which follow after those. For example, there are the commentaries by the emanation of Vajrapani, the Dharma King Suchandra; by Manjughosha emanating as the Kalki King Manjushri Yashas; by Avalokiteshvara emanating as the Kalki King Pundarika; and so forth.

However, intellectuals who do not realize this intention or those who wrongly realize it distort the meaning so much that they do not enter it even in the slightest. That which is the completely pure intention of the Bhagavan Buddha is the Dharma of the Age of Perfection. The views of the age having three parts, two parts and so forth are definitely not equal to that genuine and final view.

With regards to the degree of distortion introduced by intellectuals, during the age having three parts, three parts of the view are said to be pure while one part is distorted. Then, gradually, there arises the age having two parts where there are two parts which are pure and two parts which are distorted. This is followed by the age of degeneration in which only one part is pure. By the end of this age, all parts have become distorted. As a result of these distortions, the faults of non-realization and misconceptions arise. That is how the ages should be understood.

In the age of perfection, when the view is not veiled by any distortions whatsoever, there is the completely correct view and doctrine of zhentong madhyamaka like that which was propounded by the Omniscient Buddha from Dolpo. In brief, the view of the way things are in the age of perfection is not distorted because it does not enter into the distortions of conceptual characteristics. After the age of perfection, the gradual entrance into successive ages leading to the age of degeneration and so forth is considered the uncommon method of classification.

In the *Fourth Council*, the Buddha from Dolpo teaches:

Those who wish to enter the good path of self and other
Witness the excellent Dharma of the age of perfection, receiving it on their crowns.
From the age having three parts down, there are faults.
Like milk in a market place, the sources become contaminated.

Also:

Buddha-nature seems to be the ground of liberation.
Is it not the ground of liberation of incidental defilements?
Buddha-nature seems to be the ground of isolation.
Is it not the ground of isolation of incidental defilements?

Buddha-nature seems to be the ground of purity.
Is it not the ground of purity of incidental defilements?
Buddha-nature seems to be the ground of non-existence.
Is it not the ground of the non-existence of incidental defilements?

> *If one makes assertions like that, there are immeasurable faults.*
> *The tradition of the age of perfection lacks these defects and faults.*
> *The assertions which classify all knowable objects as things or non-things*
> *Are the tradition of the age having three parts.*
>
> *Even though the middle way of the nature of phenomena*
> *Is the most excellent object of knowledge,*
> *It is neither a thing or non-thing. Nevertheless,*
> *The explanation of a third alternative is the age of perfection.*

This tradition of the view of the age of perfection is much more exalted than all other views. The fully detailed presentation of this is not presented here. However, it should be known by way of the many details presented in the *Fourth Council* and other extensive texts written by the father, the Omniscient One Possessing the Four Reliances, and his sons.

* * *

> *The Dharma treasury of the age of perfection*
> *transforms the samsara of this world.*
> *The Buddha from Dolpo alone was skilled in its proper classification.*
> *In this great ground is glorious peace and harmony, compatible with all.*
> *If you want to enter this, then enter the complete Dharma of*
> *the age of perfection.*

2. THE UNIQUE QUALITY OF HAVING GREAT CONFIDENCE DUE TO CLEARLY KNOWING THE INSEPARABILITY OF GROUND AND RESULT

With regards to the way that actual buddhahood abides in the ground at the time of the ground, the glorious protector Nagarjuna has taught in his *Praise of Dharmadhatu*:

> *All who do not know it,*
> *Forever revolve in the three realms.*

To the expanse of phenomena,
Which abides in all beings, I prostrate and bow!

That which becomes the cause of samsara
Is purified by suchness;
Just that purity then is nirvana.
Even the dharmakaya is suchness.

As it is said here, the nature of phenomena in all phenomena—the ultimate mode of abiding—has three occasions: (1) the ground at the time of a sentient being; (2) the ground at the time of the paths of accumulation, preparation, seeing and habituation which are traversed by ordinary beings and noble ones; and (3) the ground at the time of the manifest result, buddhahood. In all three of these, the actual way of being—the ground—is always the same.

For example, for a single sentient being who cycles, there are three divisions: the time of being just a normal sentient being, the time of entering the path and the time of achieving buddhahood. While these three divisions can be categorized as different, with regards to one's own nature—buddha-nature—it is never experienced as changing.

As the Victorious One Maitreya said in the *Sublime Continuum*:

As it was before, so at a later time;
It is the changeless nature of phenomena.

Thus it is not possible for buddha-nature to have even the slightest change at any one of those times. If it were possible that our buddha-nature was different during the ground, path and result, then the ultimate result, buddhahood would necessarily be impermanent and compounded. If that were so, then buddhahood would again be nothing more than suffering. It would be no different than all of the relative phenomena of samsara. As you can see, there would be limitless faults arising from this.

Furthermore, some say that although the abiding mode is not

conditioned, it is a non-affirming negation. Such a view also enters into the above mentioned faults. So does the view that maintains without qualification that the ultimate is freedom from elaborations and so forth. These views are invalidated by scriptures such as in the *Tathagatagarbha Sutra* where it says:

> *Just as, under the house of a poor man, there might be*
> *A treasure chest that was filled with gems and gold;*
> *Since it had no deceit or arrogance,*
> *It would not say to that poor man, "I am yours."*

As is said there, even at the time of existing as a sentient being, the ground exists as the intrinsic qualities of buddhahood. For this reason, the ground and result are said to be inseparable.

Furthermore, one might think that while the buddhahood of the naturally arisen, ultimate abiding mode is meant to exist within the mindstream of a sentient being, how is it that the appearances to sentient beings of newly arisen relative phenomena could be the ultimate reality of buddhahood that is hidden within their mindstreams? If that were so, then even though the ultimate buddhahood may abide within the mindstreams of sentient beings, it is of no benefit at all. Sentient beings still suffer within the other-dependent reality, so isn't there the faulty consequence that the ultimate buddhahood—buddha-nature—is essentially powerless?

To this I would reply that it is certainly possible to think that way. However, even though a poor man may have been given a great deal of gold by another person, if he does not recognize that it is gold, then he will not enjoy the benefits that come from gold. To him the gold would seem to be useless; however it is not really like that.

Or to put it another way, even though a very kind mother might introduce her foolish child to a teacher of the path, that child might not listen and adversities might ensue. That is not the mother's fault.

Similarly, because the sky and earth are so vast, they have the capacity to accomodate all things, both good and bad alike. However, we do not blame the sky or the earth for the bad actions that we perform.

Thinking like this (that buddha-nature is powerless and so forth) is merely a misconception. Because the subtle fortune of the holy Dharma exists within all sentient beings, there are genuine signs that the nature of phenomena abides within their continuums. As Jetsun Taranatha taught in the *Wish-Fulfilling Gem of the Middle Way*:

> *Virtuous thoughts of the light of buddhahood arise.*
> *By that virtue blossoming, deluded appearances are purified as they are.*

Shantideva also taught on this in the *Bodhisattva's Way of Life* where it says:

> *Just as on a dark night, from amidst the clouds,*
> *A shining instant of flashing lightning may appear;*
> *So very rarely, by the power of the buddhas,*
> *Understanding of worldly merits sometimes arises.*

It is just as it is said there. The primordially absolute kayas and the naturally arisen pristine wisdom—clear and perfect with all the major and minor marks—abides primordially within all beings. This was proclaimed by the blessed Buddha who said in the supremely excellent *Tathagatagarbha Sutra*:

> *In all sentient beings there is the nature of phenomena like me,*
> *Existing wrapped within hundreds of afflictive states of mind.*
> *So that their nature, by all purifications that are needed,*
> *May quickly become a victorious one, the Dharma is taught.*

These words are saying that the abiding mode of buddhahood in which the ground and result are inseparable is taught along with the necessity of teaching the Dharma so that this hidden buddhahood may actually manifest. As it says in the *Angulimala Sutra*:

> *Within all sentient beings exists the limitless space of the sphere of unmade Buddhahood, adorned with the major and minor marks.*

And also in the *Abridged Hevajra Tantra*, it says:

> Sentient beings are buddhahood itself.
> However, they are obscured by incidental defilements.
> When these defilements are cleared away, they are actual buddhas.

This teaches that even though the way the mind actually abides is obscured by defilements, sentient beings are actually buddhas. The *Abridged Kalachakra Tantra* similarly says:

> If the mind is purified, it will become a lord of the victorious ones.
> What is the use of other victorious ones?

Also, in the *Sublime Continuum* it says:

> The undefiled awareness that exists within embodied beings is like honey.

And also in Nagarjuna's *Praise of Dharmadhatu*, it says:

> Within the afflictions there is primordial wisdom,
> Yet it abides like that without defilement.

In accord with what is said in the very highest of sutras, tantras and treatises, this is the highest conclusion of the reasoning of both agent and action. As it is said:

> By the path which is known as "meditation",
> What is experienced and what is attained?
> Whatever enlightenment may be,
> Like that, the desired goal is established.

What this is saying is that the defiled way things appear are abandoned by the path of cultivation or meditation. The way things actually abide—the dharmakaya—is naturally liberated, like the sun emerging from the clouds. Even though beings experience the defilements, in reality they are primordially united and conjoined within their essence. According to the Victorious One, his regent and their followers, a buddha in whom the ground and fruition are inseparable, complete with all the major and minor marks, abides primordially within the continuums of all beings.

If this is well proclaimed, then the excellent view of the age of perfection is brought forth by this unsurpassable and correct explanation. This view, which cannot be defeated, does not arise in the subsequent age having three parts and so forth. This is the extraordinary explanation that is emphasized by the glorious and victorious Jonangpas.

* * *

> *If the actual buddha does not abide as the ground,*
> *Then the buddha cannot be a permanent absolute.*
> *How could an impermanently created buddha*
> *Be anything better than a phenomena of samsara?*

3. THE UNIQUE QUALITY OF BEING PROFOUND AND FIRM DUE TO KNOWING THE TWENTY SUTRAS OF DEFINITIVE MEANING

The omniscient Buddha of Dolpo Who Possessed the Four Reliances, with clear signs of having correctly realized the intention of the Victorious One, taught a wondrous path of skilful means for the fortunate followers who were suitable to be tamed by him and in so doing, led them to realize the correct view. As it says in Jetsun Taranatha's *Root of the Middle Way of the Great Vehicle*:

> *The sutras of definitive meaning, the lords of the tenth ground,*
> *And the excellent noble ones who specified how to distinguish provisional from definitive*
> *Such as Arya Asanga who was a crown ornament of the wise ones*
> *And Arya Nagarjuna and others who revealed insight without elaborations;*
>
> *By excellently relying on their authentic speech,*
> *Abandon the foolish and deceitful words of*
> *Those who have pride and renown as the great chariots,*
> *Because they lack faith.*

As it is said there, we should depend on the unsurpassable skill of the extraordinary and distinctive teachings for how to classify what is provisional and definitive. The texts of the three turnings of the wheel of Dharma were not classified by their temporal order, but rather in terms of what was being expressed. From within the final of those three turnings, the sutras of irreversible definitive meaning—the highest and most unsurpassed sutras containing hundreds of essential points about the views and doctrines of other-emptiness, the great middle way—were gathered into one place in the great treatises that traced the original sources of these pith instructions. From those, we can establish the following list of texts:

1. The Sutra on the Tathagata Essence
2. The Dharani for Entering the Nonconceptual
3. The Sutra of the Lion's Roar of Shrimaladevi
4. The Sutra of the Great Drum
5. The Sutra to Benefit Angulimala
6. The Sutra of Great Emptiness
7. The Sutra Presenting the Great Compassion of the Tathagata
8. The Sutra Presenting the Tathagata's Inconceivable Qualities and Primordial Wisdom
9. The Extensive Sutra of the Great Cloud
10. The Sutra of Great Nirvana

These ten are known as the *Ten Sutras of the Essence* which teach the intention of the Victorious One, the essential reality that is the ultimate way things are. There are also the *Ten Sutras of Definitive Meaning* which are listed as:

1. The Perfection of Wisdom in Five Hundred Lines
2. The Answers to Maitreya's Questions
3. The Ghanavyuha Sutra
4. The Sutra on the Miraculous Concentration that Attains Perfect Peace
5. The Cloud of Jewels Sutra

6. The Great and Sublime Sutra of Golden Light
7. The Definitive Commentary on the Intention
8. The Lankavatara Sutra
9. The Ornament of the Appearance of Primordial Wisdom Sutra
10. The Avatamsaka Sutra

The meaning of these "ten sutras of definitive meaning" and "ten sutras of the essence" from the eighty-four thousand collections of Dharma of the Victorious One were then refined and clarified by the omniscient lord of Jonang, Dolpopa, through his unsurpassable wisdom. None of the common scholars of India nor Tibet had ever done this before. The excellent Sherab Gyaltsen, with his unrivalled and undefiled wisdom, also used his completely correct reasoning to refute those who other traditions held as special, great or eminent—masters such as Haribadhra, the glorious Chandrakirti and so forth. As his support he drew extensively from the teachings of the Victorious One and his regent—Lord Maitreya—so that all his points were well established.

Furthermore, from among the ten sutras of definitive meaning in which the Victorious One himself elucidated his own intention, the *Definitive Commentary on the Intention* clearly teaches that the first and middle turnings of the Dharma are both provisional in meaning. Only the final turning of the Dharma is to be considered the definitive meaning.

To establish this classification as the pith which explains the intention of the six ornaments that beautified this world such as the two Supreme Ones and so forth, we can paraphrase Dolpopa's *Mountain Dharma*. Here he says that this view and doctrine of the middle way of other-emptiness, which was resolved as the ultimate intention of the Victorious One, is an extraordinarily special teaching that everyone lacks. It contains the means for realizing the intention of the Victorious One just as it is with the arising of wondrous discriminating wisdom. Therefore if one recognizes this extraordinary and distinctive teaching as special, there will be no great loss. Knowing this is important. Thus the intention of these sutras has been clearly explained by the bodhisattvas. There is no denying it.

In addition, the most important explanation of the intention of these sutras—the main subject of the *Mountain Dharma*—shows the incredibly skilful means of the author, the omniscient king of Dharma. There, the luminous absolute in which ground and result are inseparable is presented as the naturally arisen, uncompounded primordial wisdom endowed with all supreme aspects. This presentation is drawn from a great many scriptures of both sutra and tantra and is taught through many examples with detailed explanations of their meaning. Through the many gates of his oral instruction, he provides a means for his fortunate students to actualize this realization.

Likewise in a commentary based on a student's notes for Jetsun Taranatha's *Comprehending the Commentaries on the Middle Way of the Great Vehicle*, it says:

> *Thus, in general, this teaching of the definitive meaning is taught in all the words of the Victorious One, and in particular it is taught in the principal ones of essential meaning, the ten sutras of definitive meaning and in the five most excellent treatises of the tenth level bodhisattva Maitreya.*
>
> *Those which were composed by Manjushri such as the oral instructions of the Brief Teaching Establishing the View and so forth, as well as others such as the Bodhisattva Trilogy and so forth, are the special commentaries on the intention. There are also the teachings of the Victorious One himself that clearly distinguish the provisional and definitive. Among these, the Root Tantra of Manjushri prophesies:*
>
>> *"The monk who will be named Asanga will be competent. In the meaning of the treatises and in distinguishing the sutras of many kinds. He will bestow upon the world great awareness of what is provisional and definitive meaning. He will appear to compose the doctrine."*

> *As it is said there, this subject is only entered in dependence upon the sacred writings of the excellent Noble One who abides on the third bodhisattva ground, the venerable Asanga; the writings of his brother, the master Vasubandhu, the crown ornament of all learned ones in this world and famed as a second Buddha; as well as the works of his followers, the wondrous textual tradition of the six excellent ornaments who beautified this world such as Dignaga, glorious Dharmakirti and so forth; the realizer of the insight of pristine wisdom without elaboration that was prophesied by the Victorious One, the Noble Nagarjuna, and his followers; as well as Chandragomin, who was famed as a wondrous master, Shantideva and many other holy beings.*

Moreover, it is said:

> *There were people other than those in India and here in Tibet, composers of many treatises, who were unjustifiably arrogant about being great chariots. These individuals are separate from the tradition of the actual chariots. These renowned ones were famous everywhere. However, despite their great analytical knowledge, they failed to properly understand the intention of the definitive meaning. Even though they may have possessed one aspect of discriminating wisdom, they did not possess enough merit and so they did not understand it properly. Therefore they were foolishly ignorant about the definitive meaning and even if they did understand it a little, their minds were deceptive and not straightforward. The deceitful words that they used to compose their treatises are not to be trusted and should be abandoned.*

As is taught there and other places, the definitive meaning is taught in the *Treatises of Maitreya*, Asanga's *Commentary on the Difficult Points of the Sublime Continuum*, his teachings in the *Stages of Practice*, and the *Collections of Praises* by Arya Nagarjuna. When the reality of those teachings is seen by those with unelaborated minds, the intention of the

Victorious One and his children are seen to fit like clay in a mold or a jewel in its setting. It is this genuine, ultimate intention of the Victorious One that is the view of the glorious and victorious Jonangpa.

Just as all small streams are gathered into the ocean, there is no place within the Dharma of the great vehicle and tantras that does not lead to this unsurpassable view and doctrine. Therefore it should be known as the "unsurpassable unique teaching that emphasizes the twenty sutras of definitive meaning" because it is well taught and emphasizes those.

* * *

All of the Conqueror's teachings are like churning an ocean of milk.
The treasure of its depth of meaning is like the excellent essence of butter.
Truly skilled in the twenty sutras of definitive meaning,
There are none like the Omniscient One, Dolpopa.

4. THE UNIQUE QUALITY OF BEING HARMONIOUS DUE TO CORRECTLY KNOWING THE MEANING OF THE THREE TURNINGS OF THE WHEEL OF DHARMA TO BE WITHOUT CONTRADICTION

Regarding what is provisional and definitive within the three turnings of the wheel of Dharma, the teachings of Jetsun Taranatha state in *Distinguishing the Two Modes*, "The three stages of the wheels are not classified as earlier or later in time." Following this, the Jonang do not classify whether a teaching is provisional or definitive based on the order in which they were received. Instead, they focus on what was actually said within those teachings.

For the most part, those who are proud of producing the many great doctrines of Tibet define provisional meaning as those teachings whose literal words do not accord with ultimate referents. Consequently, they make assertions that many of the Buddha's teachings are actually false words or words with a hidden intention. As Taranatha wrote in the *Ornament to the Middle Way of Other-Emptiness*:

> Most Tibetans say that in the three turnings of the wheel of Dharma,
> The first turning is false because all phenomena are taught to be truly existing;
> The middle turning is the definitive meaning because it teaches emptiness;
> The last turning is provisional because it teaches the existence of an
> ultimate.
>
> Generally speaking, not all provisional meanings are false words.
> In the stages of the path that lead to the excellent way things are,
> The teachings on the relative are provisional in meaning,
> While the teachings on the way reality exists
> Are taught as the definitive meaning and asserted by the wise.
>
> The three-fold turning of Nagarjuna,
> Asanga, and his brother are established to have one meaning.
> In the first turning, the relative is taught
> In accordance with the way it appears.
> Since analyzing for true existence, the actual way things are,
> Is not taught in that turning, these are not false words.
>
> The middle turning refutes all phenomena within samsara and nirvana,
> And all that is relative. However, the subject of whether buddha-nature
> Exists or does not is never taught and thus is not analyzed.
> Therefore, these first two turnings do not contradict the last.
>
> While the relative is primarily taught in the first turning,
> The definitive meaning is merely mentioned in the middle.
> Only in the last is the ultimate taught completely.
> Using the examples of medicine and learning the alphabet,
> This is the intended meaning, while the others are inconsistent.

THE GREAT MIDDLE WAY

Some believe that when determining the actual intention behind a text, if the *three challenges* or factors of opposition are complete, then it must be considered provisional. These three are: (1) that the text was taught for a pragmatic purpose; (2) that it has an unstated intention; and (3) that it would be false if taken literally. However, Jetsun Taranatha points out the faults of using these three criteria in his text *Ornament of Other-Emptiness*:

> *If all teachings where some phenomena is asserted are considered to be provisional in nature, then since the holy Dharma is taught to benefit all those to be tamed, then it would all have to be provisional.*

In the same text he goes on to say:

> *In the first turning, if "all phenomena are self-established" was taught, then that would contradict the Sutra of Advice to Katyayana and so forth.[1] In the middle, if the absolute space of the dharmadhatu and so forth were refuted, then that would necessarily contradict the Request of Maitreya and so forth.[2] According to those words, since the three turnings of the wheel of Dharma lack even the slightest degree of internal contradiction, the way of distinguishing the provisional and definitive is like climbing a staircase of unique teachings with wondrous and eloquent expressions. This is what allows the skilful means of pith instructions to be realized by beings. Moreover, the final turning brings forth the unique teachings that are the profound essence of the Victorious One's intended meaning. They are elucidated as the definitive meaning. That elucidation is no mere personal fabrication.*

---

1   This sutra is unusual among first turning texts in teaching the emptiness of phenomena. If phenomena were non-empty, by nature self-established, they would be eternal. However, the sutra says: "Cessation in the world, Katyayana, seen and correctly understood just as it is, shows there is no permanent existence in the world."

2   If buddha-nature were refuted, it could not be experienced and the paths from seeing to no more learning could not be entered. However the sūtra says: "Unproduced and non-arising, Without self-nature or location, Neither mental cognition, nor substance—May I realize experientially the teaching of emptiness."

As it was taught by the Victorious One himself in the *Definitive Commentary on the Intention*:

> *The Blessed Ones teach "The essence of phenomena is non-existent." They also teach, "Arising is non-existent, cessation is non-existent and from the very beginning, there is peace, the naturally complete nirvana." For those who genuinely abide in all the vehicles, they turn the third extremely wondrous and marvelous wheel of Dharma with its eloquent distinctions. That turning of the wheel of Dharma by the Blessed Ones is the unsurpassed definitive meaning that offers no opportunity for refutation.*

Then in the *Lankavatara Sutra* it also says:

> *As sick persons are given medicine by a doctor in accordance with their sickness, so too does the Buddha also teach sentient beings about the mind alone.*

In this way the teachings which distinguish between provisional and definitive are attained. As the Victorious One taught in the same sutra:

> *In the country of Beta in the south,*
> *There will be a glorious monk who is very famous.*
> *He will be called by the name of "Naga".*
> *He will destroy the biases of existence and non-existence.*
>
> *Excellently explaining my vehicle to the world,*
> *This unsurpassable great vehicle,*
> *That which establishes the ground of Supreme Joy,*
> *He will then travel to Sukhavati.*

Then in the *Manjushri Root Tantra*, it says:

> *As for the monk known as Asanga,*
> *Capable in the meaning of the treatises,*
> *He will excellently distinguish the many aspects*
> *Of the provisional and definitive meaning of the sutras.*

> *A master of teaching the knowledge of the world,*
> *He will have the disposition to write many texts.*

Also:

> *To this refuter of the doctrines of others,*
> *He who was previously a merchant and also a physician,*
> *Offering various gifts to both of these,*
> *He will be called a "man of letters" and will be renowned as a monk.*

The glorious lords of the teachings prophesied here are none other than Arya Nagarjuna and Asanga, along with his brother Master Vasubandhu. With regard to the way these brothers interpreted the Buddha's intended meaning, as it was said in Nagarjuna's *Precious Garland of the Middle Way*:

> *Just as grammarians guide people to enter*
> *Into reading subsequent letters,*
> *The Buddha teaches students*
> *Only as much Dharma as they can bear.*

In this way, with regard to those who distinguish the provisional and definitive, those are praised by the very scriptures that distinguish the provisional and definitive in accordance with how the Conqueror distinguished provisional and definitive. Those very distinctions between the provisional and definitive are the extraordinary way of distinguishing provisional and definitive in the middle way philosophy of other-emptiness of the age of perfection.

* * *

> *Through relying on the Victorious One himself,*
> *the regent and their heart sons*
> *Who distinguished which sutras were provisional and definitive;*
> *Dolpopa, the one who was supreme among those who*
> *were praised in the scriptures,*
> *Made being attached to existence laughable in this world.*

5. THE UNIQUE QUALITY OF BEING COMPLETELY FREE DUE TO REALIZING THE VIEWS OF MAITREYA, ASANGA AND NAGARJUNA AS BEING WITHOUT CONTRADICTION

The Dharma lineage of the glorious and victorious Jonang tradition possesses the supreme teachings of this great fortunate aeon and therefore does not need to rely on others. The textual tradition of the Buddha and the tenth level bodhisattva Maitreya are its authentic and trustworthy sources.

Within this tradition are the perfect teachings of the Buddha which are the unrivalled commentary on his own intention. There are also the complete commentaries by the Victorious One's regent—Lord Maitreya—who displays the pristine wisdom body of a great being, and the teachings of Asanga, who attained the third bodhisattva ground of a noble being. Asanga was praised without objection by the scriptures of the Victorious One and personally taught the cycle of the *Stages of Practice*, his commentary on the *Sublime Continuum* and so forth, in which he offered conclusive commentaries on the intention. Likewise there are the teachings of that bodhisattva's brother, the master Vasubandhu, with disciples who stretch out into an unbroken lineage of view and doctrine. It also includes the *Collection of Praises* and other treatises by the noble Nagarjuna, in which there are found great pith instructions that are like adornments on the edges.

Harmonious as one, the two supreme ones and the six ornaments that beautify the world elucidated their view and doctrines without contradiction. The blessings of their lineage and the continuity of their acceptance have never been interrupted. They abide in an unfailing succession as a continuous and unbroken lineage whose brilliant power has not decreased in the slightest. Borrowing from these various different lineages, this tradition of the Jonang is a textual tradition unrivalled by the hundreds of thousands of biases and partialities of those who take great pride in their learning. In relation to the lineage holders who possess this view and doctrine, the blessed Victorious One said in the *Descent into Lanka Sutra:*

> *Those who are dependent on mind alone*
> *Do not conceptualize external objects.*
> *Depending on appearance being non-existent,*
> *Even the mind alone is subsequently transcended.*
>
> *Depending on observation of the real,*
> *Appearance of what does not exist is transcended.*
> *If the yogin remains in mere non-appearance,*
> *Then the great vehicle will not be seen.*

In another sutra it says:

> *Victorious Ones of the past, future and also the present,*
> *As well as those of the ten directions, are nothing but this perfection.*

Also as it says in the *Brief Teaching Establishing the View* by Manjushri:

> *In the text of the Vaibhashikas,*
> *Of the Sautrantikas and the Yogacharins,*
> *A little is true, and a little is not true;*
> *But all is true within the Madhyamaka.*

As is said there, the nature of phenomena—buddha-nature—is eternally stable and changeless as the inseparable ground and result. It is the primordial wisdom endowed with all aspects, nondual with the dharmadhatu. Having a nature of pure lucidity, the three levels of existence must be just this. When it is understood that this is so, then as the lord of learned ones Gendun Chöpel rightly said:

> *Those traditions that contradict the views and doctrines of the learned ones of Madhyamaka and Yogachara, does not trust the teachings of the great sages and capable ones.*

THE EIGHTEEN UNIQUE QUALITIES

The noble one Asanga and the prophesied protector Nagarjuna—who were both praised in the sutras of the Victorious One, the perfect Buddha—distinguish the provisional and definitive meaning. As for those that think their commentaries are contradictory and so forth, Jetsun Taranatha listed a series of gradually more grievous wrong views in his *Ornament of Zhentong Madhyamaka*:

The exponents of self-emptiness, while they are proclaiming
Only the texts of Nagarjuna, are indeed in accord.
However, some maintain external objects while others deny them.
Some proclaim self-awareness and some deny it.

Some maintain the eight types of consciousness and some deny them.
Those of the foundational vehicle realize two kinds of selflessness,
Or they do not and so forth. Due to all their root doctrines
Being self-created, they quarrel.

All phenomena surely accord with mere non-existence.
However, those who follow the founders of the traditions of the two chariots,
Have unreliable minds which yield paths of their own making.

For the exponents of self-emptiness,
They say that there are no extensive commentaries
In the sutras, vinaya and abhidharma that stand on their own.
Then, after having separately analyzed the view in isolation,

When the tradition of these three baskets is explained,
Some take on the view of Vaibhashikas, some the Sautrantikas,
And some the textual tradition of the Yogachara.

The exponents of other-emptiness enter into the five treatises of Maitreya,
And the oceanlike textual tradition of Asanga and his brother.
Therefore, in their root doctrines, they are without discord.

Just as it says there, the glorious and victorious Jonang have gathered together all aspects of these many textual traditions and therefore established a stable view and doctrine that is without incongruous distortion. The structure was set up on the basis of the Victorious One's regent Maitreya and his only heart disciple, the noble one, Arya Asanga. The various textual traditions that arose from the two supreme ones and the six ornaments of the world are the final adornments.

This view of the great madhyamaka is like the very pinnacle of a temple. It represents the essential intention of an ocean of sutras and tantras of the mantrayana that are without faults of contradiction or incongruity. As the victorious one Maitreya has said in the *Sublime Continuum* along with its commentary by Arya Asanga:

> *Similarly, the undefiled awareness existing within*
> *Embodied beings is like honey.*

Then, in the *Praise of Dharmadhatu*, the glorious lord, Arya Nagarjuna says:

> *Within the afflictions, primordial wisdom*
> *Abides similarly without defilement.*

While Dignaga and his spiritual heirs say:

> *In the luminous nature of the mind,*
> *Defilements are incidental.*

As is taught in these passages and others, the single pith of the intention is the harmonious melody of the Victorious One, his regent and their followers.

* * *

> *Having discriminating wisdom by knowing the excellent explanations,*
> *Of the bodhisattvas of the tenth and third ground,*
> *The principal ones who are known as the two supreme ones*
> *and the six ornaments*
> *That beautified this world are seen to be non-contradictory.*
> *That is the excellent path.*

6. THE UNIQUE QUALITY OF POSSESSING THE PROFOUND MEANING DUE TO EMPHASIZING THE COMMENTARIES OF THE TENTH-LEVEL BODHISATTVAS ABOVE ALL OTHERS

One may ask how it is that the root meaning of this textual tradition of the Jonang accords with the bodhisattva of the tenth ground, Maitreya? In accordance with the tradition of Dolpopa's understanding of the *Sutras of the Perfection of Wisdom*, we should rely on the especially exalted traditions of explanation that accords with the way the Buddha himself taught. As a result of this approach, just because a system of explanation may be famous, that is not a good enough reason to accept it.

For example in our tradition it is said:

Phenomena of form and so forth should be explained as they are in the sutras, as being divided into three natures.

Or also as when Jetsun Taranatha wrote in the *Root of the Supreme Vehicle*:

In commenting on the line:

The lord of the tenth ground whose discourse is certain and true...

It is said:

In general we rely on all of the words of the Victorious One, but especially those which are principal—the sutras of definitive meaning, the ten sutras of the essence and so forth; the most excellent of treatises, the five treatises composed by the lord of the tenth ground Maitreya; the Brief Teaching Establishing the View taught by Manjushri; as well as the Bodhisattva Trilogy which were taught by others.

Like this, in reliance upon many holy beings one enters into the definitive meaning. However for some commentators, while they are aware of the final intention of the definitive meaning, their attitude is deceitful and they are not straightforward with how they present it. The words of treatises that are composed by such people who engage in obfuscation of the meaning are not trustworthy and should be abandoned.

Just as it is said there, those teachings which are in accord with the words of the lords of the tenth ground cast aside the textual traditions of later logicians. As it says in the *Descent into Lanka Sutra* of the great middle way:

> The excellent essence of buddha-nature
> Is not within the scope of logicians.

And also in the *Sublime Continuum*:

> The undefiled awareness existing within sentient beings is like honey.

From that single quote, the whole scope of the ground, path and fruition can be known. In order to give birth to the intended meaning of the final turning—the definitive meaning—we should not fabricate our own ideas out of presumptuous pretension. Rather we can rely on the root sources of this doctrine that have been left by the tenth-level bodhisattva Maitreya, the kalki kings of Shambhala and so forth. As Taranatha wrote in the *Ornament of Zhentong Madhyamaka*:

> Among all the collections of scriptures and commentaries of the great vehicle, since the yogachara depends solely on itself; just as the mountains around a wheel-turning king cannot be penetrated by hundreds of bandits, so too the Dharma of the yogachara cannot be overcome by the traditions of self-emptiness.

> As some of the various students of the sutras teach in accord with the Buddha's intention, their treatises are very powerful. Even if there are those who oppose them, they can still be true. Commentaries on the intention which are better than those of Maitreya will not be found in the ten directions of this world, no matter how hard one may search.

Because the Noble Nagarjuna proved this through valid cognition, as did Chandrakirti, who was prophesied in the Descent Into Lanka Sutra and he who also gave rise to the commentary where white virtue arose.³ This is also quite in accord with the auto-commentary and so forth.⁴

As for the Four Hundred⁵ and the elder protectors of the Dharma,⁶ they explained mental cognition within the Middle Way in accordance with how Chandrakirti taught; therefore⁷ while the texts of this noble father and sons indeed have a much different approach to later teachers of self-emptiness,⁸ the same established conclusions are present, even though the reasoning for them is not.⁹

The masters at the time of the father Dignaga and his spiritual sons incorporated the intentions of both Nagarjuna and Asanga. The contradictions that existed in later times between prasangika, svatantrika and so forth were not seen.¹⁰

---

3   This refers to a commentary by Master Nagarjuna's student Devashrama. This commentary on the *Root Verses on the Middle Way* from Nagarjuna's *Collection of Reasonings* is well known to be elucidated in the style of zhentong, and cannot but be so analyzed. That the entire Collection of Reasonings has been elucidated in the style of zhentong is also well known.

4   Abbreviated Tibetan title of Nagarjuna's *Auto-Commentary on the Root Verses on the Middle Way*.

5   Aryadeva's *Four Hundred Verses of Yogic Conduct*

6   Monks called the three eastern learned ones: (1) Jñanagarbha, (2) Shantarakshita and (3) Kamalashila.

7   For these and many other reasons not presented here.

8   If they are looked at superficially without analysis, there is much that is not like the later masters of self-emptiness' way of elucidating.

9   At this time, proclamations by teachers like these that the intentions of Nagarjuna and Asanga were incompatible and other such assertions of rangtong opposing the third turning existed merely as theses to be proved, rather than as reasoned proofs. Knowing that is important.

10   The noble fathers and their following sons all were without conflict. Therefore conflicts between prasangika and svatantrika madhyamaka, involving Chandrakirti and so forth, arose later.

> *Within the doctrines of the noble masters and students, since creating contradictions would have been pointless, and since disputes between prasangika and svatantrika arose only later on, and since there was no authority,[11] the view of other-emptiness was taught by Nagarjuna in his Praises and his commentaries on the Five Stages, Bodhichitta and others. Nagarjuna attained both of the intentions. as Ratnakarashanti clearly explained "The doctrines of Nagarjuna and Asanga are the same."*

Thus it is taught. Ratnakarashanti wrote commentaries on the *Perfection of Wisdom Sutras*, the *Ornament of Clear Realization* and so forth. He was a teacher of the glorious Jowo Atisha, Maitripa, Zi Lotsawa and others. He is also well known as one of the eighty-four mahasiddhas. Jetsun Taranatha refers to him as being like Shantarakshita and so forth. According to some texts which attempt to refute the yogachara position on self-awareness, he clearly explained the vehicle of discriminating self-awareness. For the proponents of self-emptiness, around the end of the disputes between prasangikas and svatantrikas, they objected to his assertion that "the absolute is not within the scope of logicians."[12]

Such proponents of self-emptiness and others say that self-emptiness is a textual tradition with sound reasoning, but that none of the treatises and those of Nagarjuna are free from contradiction with those of Asanga and his followers, who have the approach that accords with the teachings of Maitreya. Thus they put forward many attacks with reasoning which many learned ones at this time saw to be clearly and extensively unsuitable.

The original sources for the view of other-emptiness were the authoritative sources of the bodhisattvas of the tenth ground and the authentic doctrines they established were without contradiction. Like pure refined gold, teaching extensively in great detail, this distinctive view of the great

---

11   At that time there was no reason to emphasize, or even make note of, differences in doctrine, and no one with the authority to referee disputes if they did arise.

12   They held that the words were self-contradictory, since he was a logician himself. The meaning of this statement is explained elsewhere in this book.

middle way of other-emptiness is in complete accord with their sources—the writings of the tenth-level bodhisattvas.

* * *

> *The victorious Buddha, the regent of the Victorious One;*
> *Along with the Dharma Kings and Kalkis of Shambhala;*
> *And the essence of wisdom and kindness,*
> *the great beings of the tenth ground;*
> *Are all joined together here. What need is there for another path?*

7. THE UNIQUE QUALITY OF BEING INCONTROVERTIBLE DUE TO BEING SUPPORTED BY A RICH AND UNRIVALLED TEXTUAL TRADITION

The Tibetan lineages are generally considered to be independent Dharma lineages of Buddhist teachings. While they are all certainly very rich lineages, from among them all the especially rich and pure textual tradition of the glorious and victorious Jonang has a number of distinctive teachings which make it particularly unique. This is mainly due to the fact that in addition to elucidating the twenty extraordinary sutras of definitive meaning, there is also great understanding and experience of the many unsurpassable tantras in general and in particular that of the king of all tantras, the glorious Kalachakra.

In reliance upon Jetsun Taranatha's power of fathoming the entire legacy of Buddhist tantra and especially those taught in the Tibetan teachings, the Lama Thubten Gelek Gyatso composed an extensive commentary of seven volumes on Maitreya's *Ornament of Clear Realization* during the twentieth century in the eastern region of Tibet. This treatise provides instructions for the *Perfection of Wisdom*. Also, his close disciple Lama Tsoknyi composed two very great volumes on logical reasoning. The depth and breadth of these writings is incomparable and have never been produced in all of India and Tibet. With many new subjects that had never been written about before, they are unsurpassable and unique teachings.

There were many who could not initially understand the works of these two, seeing them only as a sequence of meaningless labels. However through understanding, experience and realization they were still drawn into the path. For others who wrote commentaries, this was seen as truly amazing. It meant that this textual tradition could be given to those of sharp and dull faculties alike and thus it will be remembered with gratitude until the end of samsara.

The previous two authors were unbiased in how they presented the Victorious One's teachings of definitive meaning. From the bottom of their hearts, they taught without partiality and the outcome of how they classified the teachings was truly remarkable. In one part of these teachings, Lama Tsoknyi's writings on Zhentong Madhyamaka did not fall exactly within the Jonang Tradition. This evoked a great deal of passionate debate and sometimes aggression from those with narrow minds. They certainly could not grasp the incredible outer, inner and secret qualities of Lama Tsoknyi. While his completely perfect presentation of the Buddha's teachings was definitely authentic, his critics could not see his profound and vast qualities. They could only see an external display of their own faults.

The main point of contention revolved around his assertion that in reliance upon the good qualities that arise from meditation, he could not see one difference between the views of self-emptiness and those of other-emptiness. To him they were essentially the same, without even the slightest degree of contradiction or incongruity.

However, I and those like me have thought, "How could this dry learning about conceptual labels that is like forcefully trying to stack broken stones be the ultimate nature of all things? This idea is surely harmful and could not possibly be a proper topic of explanation."

In brief, when compared to the sacred outlook and experiential realization of these two authors, someone who knows only the aspect of reasoning could not possibly characterize even the sun's capacity to shine light on

THE EIGHTEEN UNIQUE QUALITIES

— Arya Asanga —
The great charioteer who transmitted the teachings of Maitreya..

a mountain. I find it quite shameful when people who focus solely on the textual tradition of self-emptiness become filled with dissatisfaction about the teachings which unify logic and experience.

When Lama Tsoknyi passed on the qualities of his enlightened body, speech and mind to his heart son Lama Lodrö Drakpa in Dzamthang, was this not the result of a blossoming of realization and should that not be praised by all great beings from every lineage?

In the Jonang, there are a great many practitioners who after relying on this extraordinary textual tradition and using it to train on the path, are then able to realize the many distinctive teachings of the other Tibetan dharma lineages. For example, one of the distinctive teachings that is widely taught in all the lineages is that of the irreversible path of definitive meaning. It is mainly used as a foundation for then supporting each of their uncommon practices.

However, from among these the treatises of the victorious Jonang root and lineage masters have arisen from a meditative space that overflows with realization. Emerging from their experience, they did not depend upon the fixed rhythms of poetry or melodies. Therefore what use is there to even compare them with the hundreds of thousands of reasonings set forth by logicians, let alone evaluate each of their worth?

From among the extraordinary sources that were relied upon by Dolpopa, the *Stages of the Yogachara* and *Overcoming Harm to the Three Mothers* were written by Asanga and Vasubandhu respectively, both of whom were great yogins in the noble land of India. Furthermore, they both elucidated the intention of the three previously mentioned works of Maitreya, the *Bodhisattva Trilogy* and so forth.

To this day, we hear the wondrous account from the twelfth century where it is said that the mahasiddha Maitripa saw an incredible light emerging from a crack in a stupa. When he went to investigate it, he found the final two volumes of Maitreya—*Distinguishing Dharma and Dharmata* and the *Sublime Continuum*. As he took hold of them, he saw the face of the victorious Maitreya looking down on him through the clouds.

Then through his accomplishment in meditation, he gave those teachings to the brahman Sañjala who in turn bestowed the explanatory tradition to Ngok Lotsawa and the contemplative tradition to Zi Lotsawa Gawi Dorje. From then onwards, this *Contemplative Tradition of Maitreya* has become a special and direct lineage filled with incredible blessings. It is this uncontaminated and pure lineage that is now held solely within the glorious Jonang tradition and no others. Whoever has received the unblemished intention of these teachings has become incomparable and thus the lineage has remained unbroken.

As for the reason that this practice lineage has remained unbroken, it is because it has always been held as the principal view and doctrine of the Jonang and thus formed the foundation of its practice. Then over time, as the core teachings were extended by incredible commentaries such as Dolpopa's *Mountain Dharma*, it became especially exalted as the highest and most excellent of teachings.

In addition, there is also the Dharma cycle of the glorious Kalachakra with its various treatises adorned by its extraordinary view and practice instructions, as well as the lineage of oral instructions. These are an excellent and unparalleled entry into the sacred Dharma.

Moreover, as Taranatha wrote in the *Ornament of Zhentong Madhyamaka*:

The exponents of other-emptiness enter into the ocean of the five treatises of Maitreya
As well as the textual tradition of Asanga and his brother.
Therefore their root doctrines are without any contradiction
With all of the other commentaries on the scriptures of the great vehicle.

Since the yogachara texts are not dependent on others,
Just as many hundred of mountain bandits
Cannot overcome the wheel-turning king,
The texts on self-emptiness are unable to overcome these.

In this way, due to the sutras and treatises on definitive meaning, the lineage on the side of the sutras was increased by the spiritual heirs to the lineage of Maitreya. Depending on the texts of the Dharma Kings, Kalkis and so forth, their presentation of the ground, path and result which was mainly spoken about in the tantras is renowned by all as being invincible, supreme vajra speech. For example, in the *Tathagatagarbha Sutra* it says:

> The buddha-nature in which ground and result are inseparable
> Is pointed out by the ground, path and result
> Being taught completely through
> Many examples with their many meanings.

As this is so, these especially exalted and extensive texts are the basis for the wondrous and extraordinary teaching of the glorious and victorious Jonang.

* * *

Differentiating the realizations of the tradition of
the Buddha and bodhisattvas,
From the ordinary and renowned traditions of panditas and yogins,
Can only be done through a very special internal experience of the view
And not through the conceptual proofs of reasoning.

8. THE UNIQUE QUALITY OF STRENGTH DUE TO BRINGING FORTH THE POWER OF THE ABIDING MODE BY EXCELLENTLY STRIVING IN THE ESSENCE OF THE FOUR RELIANCES

All proponents of doctrine, whoever they may be, present the four reliances as important and valuable key points. At the time of entering into the way things are, rather than the four reliances being abandoned and discarded, the pith instructions say to unite with them. Within all of the writings of Dolpopa, there is not a single text that says otherwise.

THE EIGHTEEN UNIQUE QUALITIES

This excellent one, by gradually climbing the staircase of the doctrine in general, completely realized without any omission all of the essential points of what exists and what does not, what is and what is not. It was for this reason that he became very famous and instead of calling him by his given name or referring to his clan, he was known far and wide as "The Omniscient One". Through the power of his matchless understanding, he beat the drum of Dharma by which the final intention of the Victorious One is easily realized.

The perfect Buddha himself praised Dolpopa in the vajra prophecy found in the *Ushnisha of Complete Victory Sutra*, where he speaks of a holy person who will raise the victory banner of the Dharma:

In a year that is fifteen hundred distant,
In the red-faced country there will be
A monk who is like me and grasps the teachings
As a river, a heavenly tree and a beautiful garland.

His father will be famed as a lord of wisdom,
And his mother as an ornament of discipline.
In a city built on the peak of Kayo Mountain,
Their son with the name of Buddha will arise.

He will raise the victory banner of my teachings,
Sounding the Dharma conch and waving many banners.

As for the praises of Dolpopa found in this prophecy, just this is said in a great many sutras and tantras. He was indeed a great holy being, whose teachings were inseparable from the intention of the exalted Lord Maitreya, Asanga, Vasubandhu and so forth. In reliance on the power of his own understanding, he emphasized the unsurpassable teaching of the four reliances.

Regarding these four the extremely excellent sutra of definitive meaning, the *Great Nirvana Sutra*, says:

> Monks should be made to abide in four types of Dharma. What are these four?
>
> Rely on the teachings, but do not rely on the individual.
> Rely on the meaning, but do not rely on the words.
> Rely on the primordial wisdom, but do not rely on consciousness.
> Rely on the definitive meaning, but do not rely on provisional meaning.
>
> These four types of Dharma are what should be realized. However, there are not four types of beings.

In this way the four reliances are taught. To explain them further, I will now offer a brief commentary on each point. First we must enter into the teachings of the abiding mode of knowable objects. Then the established objects of those teachings should be differentiated as incidental or ultimate.

While it is necessary to analyze the abiding mode, we can examine the idea of following others who do not have reasons or (said another way) those who only appear to have reasons. For example, even though the name of an individual may be well known, that is not sufficient reason to receive teachings from that person. If the distinctions of what is good and bad are made solely on hearsay, then the danger of making mistakes is extremely great.

Even though one may have resolved what objects of knowledge to focus on, one must still determine from among those which are actually true to the nature of reality. In this case we must not get lost in well formed verbal rhetoric. Rather we should rely on abiding in the realizations of the profound and vast.

Within the context of someone who is searching for the meaning of the ultimate way things are, the mind should always rely on the primordial wisdom of the meditation of the noble ones because it is not stained by incidental defilements. The mind should not put its trust in consciousness, because it is tainted by delusive, conceptualized appearances.

When finally resolving the meaning of the ultimate way things are, it is important to understand the difference between the signifier and the signified. Provisional meanings merely express what supports the path with other provisional meanings. The definitive meaning expresses the absolute truth of how things are. Therefore one must not be mistaken about these two. The mind should not rely on provisional signifiers or relative objects which are what is signified. Instead it should rely on signifiers of the definitive meaning that signify the absolute nature of reality.

Not conforming to the mere pretense of saying one abides like that, Dolpopa Sherab Gyaltsen—the omniscient one who was prophesied by the Buddha—brought forth a superior emphasis on the four reliances. Due to this extraordinary and distinct form of teaching, he was known far and wide as "The Omniscient One Possessing the Four Reliances."

Accordingly, all of the followers and lineage holders of this exalted lord also grasped the extraordinary, unsurpassable and distinctive teaching of the four reliances as being very important. Inspired to realize it well, they were each able to reach the profound essence of the view that surpassed all others. Of those, Jetsun Taranatha was particularly recognized as a supreme practitioner of the Jonang who possessed the four reliances. He was in the truest sense the greatest of heroes, an actual bodhisattva of the tenth ground and an emanation of a Vidhyadhara. He was famed among all, not just the Jonang, as being the most precious of teachers.

Therefore because the words of the four reliances are particularly praised and their virtues are widely expressed, this extraordinary teaching of the Jonang is particularly wondrous and unique.

* * *

In Tibet, the four reliances are famous like the wind.
However, those who actually practice them are like flowers in winter.
Since Dolpopa revealed the depths of these four reliances,
Is it not time to enter into the path of these teachings?

9. THE UNIQUE QUALITY OF PURITY DUE TO ATTAINING PURE PERCEPTION BY CLEARING AWAY THE STAINS OF IMPERFECT VIEWS

With regard to the distinctive teaching that the piths of the inner and outer view should be free from grasping onto extremes, the *Root of the Supreme Vehicle of the Middle Way* says:

> From meditating on the existence or non-existence of the absence of a self of persons, the existence or non-existence of liberation from samsara can be inferred.

As it is said there, the object of attachment that grasps onto an individual self is a "person". Other than being defined as self-perpetuating, such a self must be distinguished as either existent or non-existent in accordance with the fundamental points of inner and outer phenomena. The way to distinguish those is by looking for it either within the mind or external to it. This general method is widely known.

However, in grasping onto the referent through mere words such as statements like "it is this" or "it is not this," the innermost reality of the view within the way things are is not reached. This approach is deficient because it lacks direct perception of reality and only provides a conceptual expression.

When individuals evaluate the meaning of a particular point, they are merely taking the measure of how much of it fits within the limited container of their own minds. Since this is the case, it is not easy to evaluate whether an idea is validly established in reality or what exactly the view which is being taught by others is. Keeping this in mind is very important.

Additionally, even though everyone expresses their ideas in the same language, since internal growth occurs within a person's own system of learning, an authentic person or those that follow one should not take the doctrine of others as good or bad—or better or worse—simply from reading them in a book or from stories they have heard.

Since it is all too common for people to isolate themselves and become stagnant in their own ways of thinking, there is a real danger of not being exposed to different kinds of views or beliefs. It is easy to look down upon others and lack any degree of confidence in their teachings.

For example, in Tibet from the time we are little we are taught that "outsiders" and "non-buddhists" are inferior and dominated by thick habitual propensities. The Buddhist texts themselves are filled with refutations of the views of "outsider extremists." Regardless of whether these reasonings are correct or incorrect, the effect they have had on the minds of Tibetans is to create a bias that views other wisdom traditions as low or inferior.

Adding to this, there is also a widespread belief that the view and doctrine of the victorious Jonang is filled with many faults that are similar to those of the outsider extremists and thus the Jonang are deprecated in the minds of the people. As a result, there are even those within the present Jonang tradition who reject aspects of the profound wealth of their own view and doctrine. As the three poisons of attachment, aversion and ignorance manifest in their minds, they come to hold the views of other traditions due to excessively reinforcing these compulsive ideas or simply because they seek to improve their reputation.

These critics speak about how the view and doctrine of zhentong madhyamaka with its uncommon Dharma language is mixed with non-buddhist contaminations and so forth. When they do this, their external lack of confidence reveals their inner faults. Saying such things is just evidence of the coarse attachment and aversion within the disposition of ordinary beings, as grasping any view as supreme is supposed to be abandoned on the paths of seeing and habituation.

Those who grasp onto moral discipline or the practices of tantric yoga as being the supreme attainment are equally annoying and pretentious. They miss the essential point of the very view and doctrine that they pretend to participate in. Even if they do understand the essence, while they put on the show of being great ascetics there is still a great danger that the root downfalls of mantra will arise. Therefore these deficient views that take any conceptual construct as supreme should definitely be abandoned.

People who are diligent with respect to the Jonang view and doctrine are necessarily straightforward. Unlike those who hold their view as supreme, the former Jonang masters such as Jetsun Taranatha and so forth, regardless of whether they appeared to be like outsiders, were confident in their responsibility. Thus they produced no hope nor fear to speak of. With their great confidence, they made diligent effort so their completely pure view and doctrine might be realized by others. Therefore their profound lineage of the mind became extremely liberating.

To give a good example of how their view which realizes the way things are emerges from the expanse of the mind, Taranatha himself taught that the Buddha emanated in the forms of Brahma, Vishnu, Indra, Shiva and so forth. Such teachings were meant to show that the outside extremists such as Maheshvara and so forth were in fact emanations of the buddhas and bodhisattvas.

Without getting trapped into thinking of the "outsiders" as lowly or loathsome, the incredible spiritual heritage from which our own system arose is not discarded, but instead transformed into pure view. Such is the incredible Dharma lineage of the Jonang.

Moreover, Jetsun Taranatha also wrote in the *Wish-Fulfilling Jewel of the Middle Way*:

> *If complex religious language of various different kinds*
> *Accords with scripture and reason, then it does what is desired.*

Also, Dolpopa wrote:

> *The hairs in the eyes of one grasping onto the side of attachment*
> *Are cleared away, so that they may enter into the Dharma with certainty.*

As it is said there, the mental eye of discriminating wisdom is completely opened by rejecting the narrowmindedness that grasps onto attachment, aversion and wrong views. Such a mind is then able to ascertain all of the key points of both inner and outer phenomena.

In this tradition that analyzes the profound path of authentic reasoning, it is of course necessary to establish certainty regarding the premises and key points. On the basis of that certainty, if one then practices in accordance with the instructions of one's teacher, then profound pure appearances of natural realization will definitely manifest. As it is said:

There is nothing that will not grow in the meadows of summertime.
In the yogic mind, there is nothing that is unclear.

Like this, we can think of the example of stones that can be found on remote mountains or in hidden valleys. Similarly, the experiential teachings of Shambhala which accord with the age of perfection continuously abide within the practices of the lineage like pure and refined gold. In reliance upon those, a great many past Jonang practitioners were able to achieve the union that is the great bliss of primordial wisdom. Even in this present time there are a few who abide in that realization. Similarly, in the future there will be those holy ones who maintain the zhentong view free from deceptive worldly politics so that the undefiled seeds of peaceful bliss in the minds of countless ordinary individuals may certainly grow. Because those good habitual propensities will remain where they are planted, slowly in time the enlightened activities of the sublime realm of Shambhala will ripen. As a result of this, the distinctive teaching of the Jonang clearly establishes the harvest of a future age of perfection.

* * *

Fixation on the supreme is what will be abandoned
on the path of seeing and habituation.
It makes no difference whether one is bound by chains of gold or iron.
The suffering of bondage still exists. Therefore fixation on the supreme
Must always be abandoned on the path of the Buddha's children.

10. THE UNIQUE QUALITY OF CLARITY DUE TO CLEARLY DISTINGUISHING BETWEEN THE WORDS AND MEANING OF THE TWO TRUTHS

In his *Sun that Illuminates the Two Truths,* Dolpopa writes:

> *Since the relative is without truth, it is self-empty.*
> *Its appearance does not appear to primordial wisdom.*
> *Moreover, since the absolute actually does exist,*
> *It is not empty of itself, it is empty of that which is other.*

As it is said there, all phenomena which appear to the eight collections of consciousness are empty of true existence. They are relative truth. The genuine objects of the noble ones' primordial wisdom is not empty of its own nature; therefore it is ultimate truth. The support for that—the union of the great primordial wisdom and the inseparable sphere of the Dharmadhatu—is also ultimate truth.

The various apparent objects of consciousness are relative truth. These include all phenomena on the side of the all-encompassing afflictions and samsara, as well as everything on the side of incidental liberation—all of the collections of temporary high status which are included within the paths of accumulation, preparation and so forth.

Everything that is conditioned is empty of true existence in the sense of an "emptiness" that is the mere absence of a non-affirming negation. As that is called relative truth in this system, how could it be absolute? The oral instructions from the lineage of the Kalkis are confident that those who maintain such an emptiness as absolute truth, along with the specifics of that view, have created a great distance with the actual state of reality; like the difference between heaven and earth.

When the textual tradition of zhentong madhyamaka is analyzed closely again and again, the intention of the buddhas will certainly be attained. If this were not true, then the ultimate way things are would be classified as an emptiness of a conceptual non-affirming negation, and would also be classified as a freedom from all elaborations since it is a mere absence. With such a form of emptiness, then the ultimate way things are is reduced to nothingness. Therefore it cannot be anything at all.

An ultimate like that, other than being merely a mentally projected non-affirming negation, is not something that can be realized in experience. As Taranatha wrote in his *Wish-Fulfilling Jewel of the Middle Way*:

> It is not the emptiness of not existing at all.
> If it were just that, then it would simply be untrue.
> For that reason it could not be realized in experience.
> Conceptual "realization" is simply conceptual abstraction.
> Asserting that is therefore useless.

As he says there, different kinds of invalidating reasonings like those mentioned previously fall like rain. Many who are arrogant about their doctrines being correct proclaim in lofty language that their view of this ultimate experience is free from the four or eight extremes of elaboration and so forth. However, when their view is explained in detail, for all of its superior manner, it is fundamentally no different from a view where the support—the fundamental reality of the way things are—is self-empty by way of a non-affirming negation. The reason we can be sure it is a non-affirming negation is because when the two kinds of self are negated, no phenomena at all can be presented that remain after the negation.

Furthermore, if that elaboration which is supposed to have been negated is then negated as well, then you simply create another conceptual elaboration. Regarding this, Sakya Pandita has said:

> If a better view exists than freedom from elaboration,
> That view has elaboration. In a teaching like that,
> After non-affirming negation negates what is to be negated,
> If what is to be negated still exists,
> Not free from elaboration, it has elaboration.
> The reasoning for this is not difficult to see.

While he says that a reasoning would exist, would this not create an infinite regress? An attempt may be made to separate the four, eight or other extremes of elaboration, thinking that they could be beneficial for mediation or study. For a beginner—an ordinary being all too familiar with the viewpoint of grasping selfhood and characteristics—wrong views are endless. To negate these degenerated views would indeed be beneficial. However, in accordance with the view that the ultimate is not free from self-emptiness, even though many relative proliferating elaborations will be cut off, it is always mistaken to believe that the true nature of reality—the way things actually are—will be apprehended by that.

While many Tibetan texts on madhyamaka may boast about how high "elaboration" and "freedom from elaboration" may be, all their explanations undoubtedly boil down to saying that the ultimate way things are is self-emptiness.

Consider this in detail. For each text's object to be negated, aside from merely saying that there is freedom from their elaborations, there is no other meaning at all. When that is said, because it is easy to understand, mere freedom from—or separation from the elaborations of the relative objects of consciousness—is merely given the label "ultimate truth." If, on the other hand, you did not even say that much and you identified it as existing as a mere label, then even though you proclaimed that it was empty of true existence, in reality you would be a proponent of other-emptiness.

Why don't we consider a different way of speaking. When referring to the genuine way things are that is free from all conventional elaborations, just that should be known to exist as limitless ultimate elaborations. If one does not know this due to attachment to the idea of freedom from elaborations, then the ultimate way things are will become nothing other than an absence of elaboration which has no way of existing. The reason for this is because those who proclaim that ultimate reality is self-empty are thereby proclaiming that it is non-existent. If, however, we posit that it is empty of other, then the ultimate would not become non-existent in the way that it does if you posit it to be empty of self.

In that style, Jetsun Taranatha wrote in his *Wish-Fulfilling Jewel of the Middle Way*:

> *Emptiness analyzed by inferential reasoning*
> *And non-conceptual resting in the relative as it is,*
> *Are mere abstractions and actual perception respectively.*
> *Ultimate suchness is not a mere mental abstraction.*
>
> *Meditating on the nature of the mind, buddha-nature,*
> *And the special phenomena which are the Conqueror's qualities are two.*
> *If the non-conceptual mind gathers these principal points,*
> *That is the supreme path of the Sugata, the definitive meaning.*

What this is saying is that the definitive meaning, the true essence of all things, cannot be dealt with by an inferential reasoning that analyzes merely for the presence or absence of freedom from elaborations. Some may try to position their view as the most supreme using lofty language to claim that ultimate truth is both free from extremes and the inseparability of appearance and emptiness, the inseparability of luminosity and emptiness, or the inseparability of awareness and emptiness and so forth. Whichever way we choose to phrase it, these sorts of incompatible assertions are simply just a bouquet of falsehood. Such statements are just nice sounding words. Except as mere verbal obscuration, their essential point cannot be understood in any great detail.

I feel very strongly about this. However, if there are people who are skilled at expression within those traditions, then it is really important that they come forward now and clearly explain this disparity.

Then there are also others holding a view of a non-affirming negation, an affirming negation or neither of the two, who say that the ultimate is free from all assertions. Consequently, they say that they make no assertions of existence or non-existence such as "this is" and "this is not" and so forth. This view arises from teachings such as those in the *Root of the Middle Way of the Great Vehicle* where it says:

Through non-assertion, deception is obstructed.

And further explained by Taranatha in the *Essence of Zhentong Madhyamaka*:

In particular, when the prasangikas are presenting their own system of classification, they try to avoid disputes with others by saying that they make no assertions at all.

If this is the case, then wouldn't the very power of language be made weak? Wouldn't promises be without confidence? Wouldn't logical arguments arise from nothing? How is it that such faults could be present for non-valid reasons? Though it is possible to always abide in non-assertion, asserting, "I am without assertions" is unnecessarily incoherent. If this is asserted by those who understand assertions, then wouldn't people claiming that they make no assertions simply be laughable in accordance with worldly conventions?

Furthermore, when something with elaboration is said, giving an answer and pretending that it is without elaborations is not good. Neither is manifesting a continuous flow of words with elaborations or those having the nature of elaboration from within a state in which a lack of elaboration has been resolved.

When those who are not without elaboration claim that they are, there is the fault of self-contradiction. For many such reasons, rather than the traditions holding doctrines like these, isn't it more effective and straightforward to classify the ultimate in the way that accords with the zhentong madhyamaka of the Jonang?

As for this explanation, just as in many views and doctrines that do not fall into bias, there are concluding summaries to produce understanding. If an ordinary person such as myself were to attempt to explain just what is known and what is being analyzed, then I would say that upon analyzing as much of the intention of the Victorious One's words as possible, the zhentong philosophy of the victorious Jonangpas relies on a way of individually distinguishing the two truths. With its genuine power, this seems to be an extraordinary and unrivalled unique teaching. For those who disagree with me and are offended by these statements, please open your mind and forgive me, for I don't have anything more to offer you.

* * *

For the two truths, the meaning of "truth" is distinct,
Because the way things are and the way things appear are also distinct.
Their purpose and their effects are also distinct.
Saying "the two truths are united" is merely a poetic device.

11. THE UNIQUE QUALITY OF BEING UNDELUDED DUE TO BRILLIANTLY DISTINGUISHING BETWEEN SAMSARA AND NIRVANA

Now with regard to the unique quality of skilfully distinguishing between samsara and nirvana, Dolpopa wrote in the *Fourth Council*:

Samsara and nirvana are not two separate kingdoms.
The apparent is samsara and the empty aspect nirvana.
Even the meaning of "inseparable samsara and nirvana"
Are asserted by some.

After identifying the faults of his opponents, he then establishes his own position by saying:

If it is consciousness, it is not the ground of primordial wisdom.
Primordial wisdom and consciousness are like light and darkness.

This is also echoed by Jetsun Taranatha in his *Root of the Great Vehicle*:

Consciousness and wisdom are individual kingdoms.
The relative and ultimate have their own modes of truth...

As taught there and other places, the objects of the eight collections of consciousness are the phenomena of samsara. On the other hand, the objects that appear to the mind that perceives the excellent primordial wisdom of the ground of everything are the phenomena of nirvana. Such is the distinction between samsara and nirvana. When it is not like that, as Dolpopa said in the *Fourth Council*:

> *The age of three parts and onwards, depending on their faults,*
> *Say that everything is empty of itself,*
> *And also say self-emptiness is the ultimate.*
>
> *They say that even the ultimate is empty of itself,*
> *And also that conceptual thoughts are the dharmakaya.*
> *They say that the five poisons are primordial wisdom,*
> *And that dualistic consciousness is buddhahood.*
>
> *They also claim that karmic appearance is buddhahood.*
> *As buddhahood is explained as emptiness of names,*
> *Buddhahood is explained as forever nonexistent.*
> *They say that ultimate buddhahood is nonexistent!*
>
> *It is said that both the two truths have but a single nature.*
> *It is said that samsara and nirvana have one nature.*
> *It is said that the objects of abandonment and their antidote have a single nature*
> *And that what is cleansed and the ultimate ground are also one.*
>
> *The origin of karma and suffering, this painful cycle of existence,*
> *Can never be known as buddhahood; merely as samsara.*
> *While those who explain these things have not fully mastered this subject,*
> *They still bestow information in the form of offering many elegant words.*

Just as it is said there, no matter how elegantly these ideas are taught by various renowned teachers, in the end they do not address their fundamental faults. Moreover, when one is not able to offer answers to these refutations and yet still claim that it is good to think this way, then it would be much better that they show restraint.

According to their approach, samsara and nirvana have no divisions of good to be accepted and bad to be rejected. If this is true, then making effort on the path of liberation would be utterly pointless. Such an idea is a great hindrance toward developing positive aspirations to strive on the path, gather the accumulations, purify the obscurations and so forth. Even just a few of these activities might enable one as a bare minimum to at least improve one's conditions within one's relative samsara.

For these reasons, even though the mind can give rise to the aspiration that strives for "the final abiding mode of the ultimate," if that idea is grasped with a non-affirming negation as being self-empty, then the profound idea "how can the innermost mind have a firm and stable nature?" is extremely important.

In general, the Jonang also proclaim and accept that ultimate reality has no divisions in its own nature, and is empty of that which is to be abandoned, accepted and so forth. However, at the time of resolving the view in experience, if the two truths are grasped as one and inseparable then there is a very great danger that one's approach will simply be a cause for further bewilderment.

The deceptive phenomena of the relative are entirely obscured. As such they have the nature of suffering, falsity, untruth and existing adventitiously. However, when analyzed they do not exist at all in the ultimate and therefore are considered to be deceptive phenomena. Ultimate liberation—the great nirvana—must necessarily be explained as the opposite of that. It must also be explained that it is necessary to explain the ultimate in that way.

Other doctrines repeat again and again that both samsara and nirvana are empty of their own natures. Then upon further explanation, the two truths are presented to be united without accepting or rejecting. The previous explanation of how the ultimate is both existent and non-deceptive is suppressed.

The view of anyone who tries to explain ultimate truth in that way will necessarily be unstable and unreliable. This kind of explanation involves many contradictions and incongruities that will cause bewilderment in practitioners. There is a very real danger of their being left like blind men lost in the middle of an open plain, without any profound and stable point of reference.

When the Jonang view is resolved, the two truths are correctly distinguished and divided. When we engage in hearing, contemplation and meditation; and also when we explain the ground, path and result, they are maintained as exclusive. In no context are they ever mixed. Therefore, this extremely unique approach is superior to others in this respect.

Furthermore, for the Jonang all conceptual phenomena are included within the side of samsara and are therefore resolved to be groundless. On the other hand, whatever is included within the ultimate reality, since it exists from the perspective of the appearance of yogic primordial wisdom, is classified as nirvana and inseparable from the result. As Dolpopa wrote in the *Fourth Council*:

> *The experience of those who have yoga is nirvana.*
> *Those who do not divide these into two separate kingdoms;*
> *Appearance and emptiness are made into samsara and nirvana.*
>
> *But if everything that appears is relative and samsara,*
> *Ultimate appearances are thus relative and samsara.*
> *If everything that is empty is absolute and nirvana,*
> *Everything self-empty is absolute and nirvana.*

When the fault of saying that samsara and nirvana are indivisible has been abandoned, then the boundaries between samsara and nirvana can be well distinguished. This is the highest teaching of the extraordinary and glorious Jonangpa.

* * *

> *Samsara is suffering and nirvana is peace and bliss.*
> *Their equality on the path, I swear is non-existent.*
> *Ultimate fruition is opposed to that union.*
> *Therefore distinguishing samsara and nirvana is utterly crucial.*

12. THE UNIQUE QUALITY OF PENETRATING TO THE DEEPEST MEANING DUE TO CLEARLY DISTINGUISHING BETWEEN EMPTINESS AND THE GROUND OF EMPTINESS

As for the distinction between the ground of emptiness and empty phenomena, the *Fourth Council* teaches:

> In the supreme and especially exalted teachings of the age of perfection,
> The ground of emptiness is the space-like primordial wisdom of the ground of everything.
> The cloud-like incidental defilements are what are to be purified.
> That which purifies is the wind-like inexhaustible truth of the path.
> The result of purification is the result of separation.
> This is like the sky being cleared of all clouds.

What this says is that the ground of purification is the ultimate luminous buddha-nature, non-dual primordial wisdom endowed with all supreme aspects. Just this is the inconceivable, authentic nature of phenomena. That which purifies is like the wind, purifying all of the cloud-like obscurations of both afflictions and cognition. This is what it means to practice Dharma and to no longer be reborn into suffering. When this occurs, the ground of purification like a clear blue sky is revealed as permanent and immutable. How then could changeable phenomena ever be the ground of purification?

Otherwise it should be sufficient to explain how some perspectives view them as equal by way of the example. That the cloud-like accumulations of defiling obscurations—which are the objects to be purified—are impermanent and temporary can be understood from their meaning. Other than this, there is no need to even consider the many aspects of suffering and so forth. Similarly, for that which purifies—the inexhaustible wind—other than the truth of the path being a cause for purification, we need not think about many other aspects.

As a result of there being a cause of clearing away the clouds, when the clouds are cleared away the sky looks different. Other than this, we need not think about the many factors involved. Though the sky appears to be obscured by the clouds that are white, black, yellow and so forth, in actuality no such differences in qualities arise at all. Similarly, the primordial ground—the buddha-nature in which ground and result are inseparable—is the ground of emptiness. If that is known, then we are liberated from our ignorant delusion.

Regarding the way we can become supreme, Jetsun Taranatha wrote in his *Wish-Fulfilling Jewel of the Middle Way*:

> *What is called a vase never existed at all.*
> *The appearance of a vase is merely a delusive appearance.*
> *What remains of this is non-dual primordial wisdom.*
> *That is the swastika of eternally stable peace.*
> *As the dharmadhatu of vases is like that,*
> *So too is the dharmadhatu of pillars and so forth.*

Like this, there is the ground of emptiness of the ultimate and the empty phenomena of the relative. In this profound view and doctrine, because their characteristics are clearly distinguished, excellent and superior discriminating wisdom does not mix up concepts such as the ground of emptiness (dharmata) and the empty phenomena (dharma).

Other views and doctrines fall into biases such as holding the unqualified view that all phenomena which are included within the two truths must be empty, or that they are the same as the ground of emptiness. Such views and doctrines do not arise from realization. This view and doctrine of the ultimate definitive meaning that rejects such wrong conceptions is the unsurpassable and distinctive teaching of the proponents of other-emptiness.

The ultimate way things are is buddha-nature. It has many characteristics such as being permanent, all-pervasive and so forth. As Taranatha wrote in his *Commentary on the Supreme Vehicle*:

Because it is unborn it is always endowed with the qualities of suchness.
It is deathless because it is indestructible.
It has the quality of peace because it is without the harm of sickness.
It has the quality of a swastika[13] because it does not age.

Because the dharmadhatu is eternal suchness, because it is unborn and stable,
Because it does not have the destruction of death,
Because it is peaceful and without sickness
And because it is the eternal swastika, it is ageless.

The nature of phenomena—suchness—is always immutably the nature of phenomena. At the time of the ground it is just like this and then later at the time of the result it is also just like this. However, at the time of the ground the dharmadhatu is associated with faults and its assembly of enlightened qualities are obscured. In contrast, at the time of the result these former faults are abandoned and therefore its qualities manifest.

One may object by asking, "Since these qualities are newly attained at the time of the result, isn't the dharmadhatu different to what it was before? Doesn't it change?"

To this I would reply, no it does not. The assembly of faults such as the afflictions and so forth are by nature unestablished. As they are merely temporary and incidental, the essence of the dharmadhatu has never actually been covered by them. The ultimate qualities, the ten powers of a buddha and so forth, are not newly attained by meditation on the path. They have existed intrinsically in the dharmadhatu from the very beginning.

---

13   Here the word "swastika" refers to the Tibetan term "yung.drung" where yung refers to being eternal and drung refers to stability. This is how it is traditionally used.

The fact that we perceive defilements to be present before and that enlightened qualities are absent is merely due to the fact that the true nature of phenomena is currently masked by the obscurations of a conceptual mind. This reality is only from the viewpoint of such a samsaric mind. In reality, the dharmadhatu has primordially never been covered by defilements. It has always been the naturally realized ultimate reality in which defilements are naturally abandoned and enlightened qualities are naturally possessed.

As for the meaning of being all-pervasive, we can think of the example of space. Even though it has never had the thought, "I should pervade everything," intangible space naturally permeates all external and internal things. It pervades everything. Similarly, the luminous nature of the mind is primordially free from proliferating elaborations. Therefore, this undefiled space can go into all pure and impure phenomena, pervading them without difference.

Only the distinctive teaching taught by the proponents of other-emptiness possesses the wondrous special insight expressed by words such as this:

"Phenomena are not empty, only true existence is empty.
By everything being empty, everything is free from the extremes of elaboration—
Not existent, not non-existent, free from assertions and so forth."
Not knowing the difference between the ground of emptiness and
The phenomena which are empty within it is a fault.

* * *

From knowing incorrectly, partially or very well
That nirvana is the ground of emptiness and samsara is empty phenomena,
A view that is incorrect, partial or very correct will arise.
Only through the view of the age of perfection
will this be completely realized.

13. THE UNIQUE QUALITY OF BEING UNMISTAKEN DUE TO KNOWING WHAT IS PRIMARY AND SECONDARY IN THE SUTRAS AND TANTRAS

Regarding the unique quality of developing competence in how to unite and divide what is primary and what is secondary in the sutras and tantras, in speaking about what is primary Jetsun Taranatha wrote in his *Ocean of Victorious Aspiration*:

> *The ultimate meaning of sutra is zhentong madhyamaka*
> *And the ultimate meaning of tantra is vajra yoga.*
> *Grasping the pith of the path links one's view with meditation.*
> *May all the gates of the Dharma be fully clarified.*

This teaching praises the clarity of the scriptures of the peerless Victorious One, the perfect Buddha. When the excellent and all knowing one Dolpopa Sherab Gyaltsen first went into retreat at Jonang, all the thoughts and conduct of the dharma practitioners in that place had the quality of deep meditation. He was greatly inspired by those yogins of liberation who were confident in their realization. He reflected that in this place, there was no way not to practice. From that moment forth, all of the sacred assemblies of his followers would hold the pure and precise conduct of individual liberation. They gave themselves fully to the peerless efforts of the foundational discipline so they would never cover themselves with even subtle transgressions or downfalls. Internally they were extremely mindful to uphold their vows of bodhichitta. Leading by example, Dolpopa himself did not eat meat throughout his life. That this would have been very difficult to follow in those times can be understood from many stories.

Nevertheless, the followers of Dolpopa practiced in accordance with the union of sutra and tantra. Their view was in accord with tantra, while their conduct was performed in accordance with the sutras. This approach was known as "the yogic discipline of mantra." With the practice of the three trainings, they did not engage in improper behaviour and so were able to achieve the realization of the great and secret mantra ripening from within.

Countless great beings living in Jonang entered into the highest levels of tantric practices and paths. This extraordinary place of practice where those holy ones lived was the glorious mountain retreat of the Jonang. Rather than practicing in other remote places, such as in caves that even birds could not reach, the assembly of students of these holy ones who practiced there were shining examples of this approach.

In brief, regarding the accomplished masters of the Dharma lineage of the Jonang, Jetsun Taranatha described their incredible merit and capacity to abide in the middle way free from the two extremes when he wrote in the *Root of the Middle Way of the Great Vehicle*:

> *If this way is realized, so is all of the great vehicle.*
> *If not, then one falls over the cliffs of eternalism or nihilism.*
> *Through the benefit of having great merit, this will be understood.*
> *By those with excellent minds, this will surely be attained.*
>
> *A life that abandons the two extremes is the path of the middle way.*
> *Nor does conduct err in the middle between accepting and rejecting.*
> *In meditation, the union of shamatha and vipashyana is the middle way.*
> *All occasions of the view are joined to that middle way.*

Thus when the view, meditation and conduct are completely correct, then actions are not wasted from the perspective of the view. From the perspective of actions, the view is not something irrelevant. Sutra and mantra are united in practice, so that all aspects are mastered without needing to rely on other sources.

Knowing the piths of what is primary and secondary; knowing how quarrels over doctrines and Dharma lineages can destroy the bridges for those practices which ripen and liberate; knowing the destructive actions that confine us in a cage of worldly politics; and knowing how the trickery of Dharma lineages can be deceptive—a great many yogins devoted themselves single-pointedly to the teaching of the irreversible definitive meaning. Even in the present, there are many beautiful ornaments living in the land of snows who embody this special wealth and who abide with contentment in their pledges.

One may then object by saying, "What the Jonang claim is that we proponents of self-emptiness remain locked in the trap of the eight worldly dharmas and other deceptive meanings of samsara. Therefore it follows that we will never be liberated and that we are unsuitable for liberation through practice and realization."

To this I would reply that there are heavy burdens of deception and envy that will inevitably come to those who strive for the eight worldly dharmas. Furthermore, in the eyes of worldly people, authentic Dharma practitioners have no value and they are not revered within society. Therefore it is clear to see the heavy price that is paid by indulging in the eight worldly dharmas.

Nevertheless, for yogins who abide among the snow mountains, there are those who hold completely pure discipline in accordance with the sutras. Countless such yogins who have realized the essential points of the view of mantra have existed in the past and continue to exist nowadays. Therefore, in this world it is a unique quality of an unsurpassable good result that they are able to distinguish between what is primary and secondary and thus unite the teachings of sutra and tantra.

* * *

The thoroughly complete sutras and tantras are
for the sake of perfect buddhahood
And nothing else. Therefore, their purpose is without contradiction.
If any contradictions whether they be grave, slight or indeed absent
Are known as mere mental distinctions,
then the actual meaning will be realized.

14. THE UNIQUE QUALITY OF BEING ROOTED IN PRACTICE DUE TO KNOWING THAT THE PROFOUND MEANINGS OF BOTH SUTRA AND TANTRA ARE WITHOUT CONTRADICTION

Currently in this world, those who say they have no faith in spiritual systems seem to spurn worship and devotion. But is this true? Do they really have no faith? Maybe they are uncertain about what to have faith in or simply cannot be bothered developing it.

From among the great many who say they do have faith in spirituality, those who have reasoned faith based on specific views and doctrines are few, whereas those who have faith without them abound. Also among those who do have views and doctrines, those whose minds are satisfied with just their own view and doctrine are many. Furthermore, when they are not respectful of other traditions, when it comes to studying them they are like sheep being herded by shepherds and are not able to study without bias.

In brief, among the seven or eight billion people on this planet, those who are able to connect profound views and doctrines to spiritual practice are exceedingly few. Among those, the ones who actually know how to clearly distinguish the two truths are even more rare. Those who know how to classify the three natures of imputed, dependent and thoroughly established are still fewer, even though that doctrine is posited by both the chittamatrins and the madhyamakas. Even more rare than all of those are the ones who know the tradition of the three natures in accordance with the extraordinary definitive meaning of the age of perfection, where the provisional and definitive are clearly distinguished.

The reason for this is easy to know. The higher the sacred Dharma, the oral instructions and so forth may be, the more merit is required to be able to realize them. Those who know this fact are therefore as rare as stars in the daytime. To give an example, consider that while those who know the way of explaining the profound meaning of both sutra and tantra are rare, their existence is still possible.

Those who have given birth in their hearts to the profound meaning of sutra and tantra and also have the good fortune of it ripening in their own mindstream are so very rare that people don't even try to refute it. For example, think about the first turning of the wheel of Dharma, by which those who struggle with what to abandon and what to adopt have the knowledge and ability to simply suppress incidental afflictive states of mind. By doing that, it is very hard to follow the scriptural instructions on how to uproot these propensities from their minds. Likewise, even though the selflessness of phenomena is not directly perceived, they do achieve an inferential understanding by way of the nine examples of illusion. Because this is only an indirect cause for realizing the selflessness of phenomena, this realization is difficult to know.

In the middle turning, the bodhichitta of the Great Vehicle and the four means of attracting others are generated. While the six perfections and so forth are taught, those who actually know ultimate bodhichitta and how it is explained in the commentaries are extremely few. Similarly, it is exceedingly rare to find those who are able to understand that the two forms of selflessness—which are described in the sutras as being endowed with the potential for displaying all manifestations—are actually non-existent.

Therefore when it comes to the highest view and conduct of the sutra tradition, those who know the phenomenal world as purity and equality are very few. If one then looks from a superficial and external perspective, sutra and tantra would appear to be unrelated. Nevertheless, other than those who have the ability to realize the profound topics that are the key points of the view, meditation and conduct from the perspective of the sutras, we can be confident that there is not even a single person connected to such people.

Still, if these key points are known and realized, then the two intentions of sutra and tantra are seen to exist without a single contradiction. But who knows this? It is very hard to identify them among sentient beings.

The number of people within each Dharma lineage who know this truth is certainly unknown. However, if such knowledge is explained in terms of the view and doctrines of those very lineages, other than the Jonang, it would be very hard to say if the other Tibetan schools actually fall into this category.

The reason for this is that in the regions where the Tibetan lineages have spread, those who hold all of them say that the ultimate way things are is that which is to be attained. They undoubtedly call it "the level of buddhahood." The Victorious One himself, the perfect Buddha, taught in various sutras and tantras that this ultimate is called "buddha-nature." However, when it comes to the commentaries on the meaning of "buddha-nature," Jetsun Taranatha wrote in his *Commentary on the Middle Way of the Great Vehicle*:

> *In general, here in Tibet there are three principal approaches to identifying buddha-nature. There is the explanation of the great translator Ngok who said that the Sublime Continuum, although it is a provisional commentary on the intention of the final turning of the Dharma, is very profound.*
>
> *According to what he says, buddha-nature is identified there in terms of the emptiness of a non-affirming negation. If so, then the final turning is no more profound than the middle one because it is without distinction in being principally taught as a mere non-affirming negation.*
>
> *The great Sakya Pandita says that the fundamental intention in identifying the essence is to identify it as an emptiness. He clearly says that the essence is mere emptiness without proliferating elaborations. However, in his Supreme Differentiation of the Three Vows, his tradition is not clearly presented. The great Butön identifies the essence with the all ground consciousness. There are many teachings such as these. However, when*

the essence has been identified in this way, whatever assertions and denials there may be, and whatever may be said about material things and inner awareness in the relative; buddha-nature cannot be truly established by direct experience as the inseparable space of the dharmadhatu and awareness. This is deluded.

However, in the Jonang's zhentong madhyamaka of the age of perfection, there is a single dharmakaya in which ground and result are inseparable. In the glorious Kalachakra, this is taught as the essence which is endowed with all supreme aspects of the deity, mantra, mudra, samadhi and so forth. It is also described in the guru's oral instructions that this same buddha-nature truly exists in practical experience as the inseparable awareness of the dharmadhatu. It has the clear and stable nature of empty bliss.

Therefore the view that the sugatagarbha is merely freedom from proliferating elaborations, merely neither existence nor non-existence, merely freedom from all assertions and so forth, cannot be reached or fathomed. That is made completely clear when view, meditation and conduct are put into practice.

The reason for this is because other views and doctrines conceptually grasp onto characteristics. Even though they are striving for freedom from elaborations, their form of emptiness still enters into the elaboration of "self-emptiness." Thus rather than reaching the ultimate freedom from extremes, their ultimate possesses all the same extremes as the proliferating elaborations of the relative.

However, since the view, doctrines and practices of the Jonang are especially exalted, there are a great many favourable conditions which give rise to the good fortune of being able to realize the profound secret meaning where the sutras and tantras are seen to be without contradiction. These causes and conditions exist within the nature of the ripened fruit.

They are not found within the shifting discursive thoughts of learned ones' conceptual assertions.

On the contrary, when practitioners enter into the glorious gate of the Jonang practice tradition, from the very moment that the student's mind first begins to be purified, in reliance upon the nurturing guidance of the guru there is a profound, secret and skilful explanation of how the sutras and tantras are not contradictory. Thus they are trained to not enter a path of merely preparing for fulfillment, but instead they strive for the experiential enjoyment of the actual thing. In this practice tradition that focuses on the actualization of the final goal, practitioners are not entering into the path completely overwhelmed by the worldly dharmas. Instead their continuums are already pure to some degree by being cleansed of the world's hypocrisy and so forth. For this reason, as they practice the sacred Dharma they have the good fortune to experience and realize the various paths and levels of attainment.

Merely presenting a conceptual view that the sutras and tantras are non-contradictory is not enough. For the Jonang, this non-contradiction is naturally realized through the view, meditation and conduct. This can be illustrated by the life stories of the holy ones of the past and I can attest to it even in my own minor experience. When the view and conduct of the sutras and tantras are grasped as being distant from each other, then there is a lot of space for the eight worldly dharmas, hypocritical pretensions and people who enjoy showing off with beautiful displays. Though it is possible for people to express foolish blind faith towards such people, one should never be concerned with what others think or say. When one traverses the path of one's own experience, then one is capable of further knowing and realization.

Among all of the unique qualities of this tradition, this one of experientially realizing the profound meaning of the sutras and tantras as being completely without contradiction is especially wonderful. Those who do not realize this never actually realize the correct intention of the sutras and tantras at all. It is as Taranatha once wrote in the *Wish-Fulfilling Jewel of the Middle Way*:

> *Whether you are capable or foolish,*
> *Whether you have power or do not,*
> *Whether your conduct is good or bad,*
> *If you strive like this, then the great goal will be attained.*
>
> *Those who are arrogant from the knowledge*
> *Displayed in teaching, debating and composition,*
> *Stubborn and hypocritical in their finely detailed projects,*
> *Venerating coarse behaviour and the practice of resounding the syllable*
> *PHAT, do not realize this profundity and fall off the precipice.*
>
> *As for this doctrine, the meaning of all the sutras and tantras*
> *Are explained and arise as experience in the mind.*
> *The intention of all the exalted noble ones is also like this.*
> *Previously non-existent, these excellent sayings have no contradiction.*

As is taught there, without realizing the non-contradiction of the intended meaning of the sutras and tantras, the actual realization of our practice will be limited. Practitioners will be incapable of traversing the path of the noble ones and so forth. Having seen the great significance that the Jonang place on knowing how to practice within this non-contradiction of sutra and tantra, I felt it important to explain here.

* * *

Realizing sutra and tantra are without contradiction is no mere slogan.
Realization through inference and those through direct perception
Are not on the same level when referring to authentic realizations.
Authentic realization is only non-conceptual realization.

15. THE UNIQUE QUALITY OF HAVING AN INTIMATE APPROACH DUE TO EMPHASIZING A CLOSE RELATIONSHIP BETWEEN MASTER AND DISCIPLE JOINED WITH PRACTICAL EXPERIENTIAL GUIDANCE

I have been very fortunate to have had the opportunity in my life to experience a little of the practices of all the great Tibetan Dharma lineages. As such, having practiced both the preliminaries and the main practices, I have been able to establish a few deeper propensities.

In accordance with my experience, I have noticed a significant difference in the relationship between master and student within the Jonang tradition versus what I observed in other Dharma lineages. If I were to merely look from the outside, it is possible to see that the Jonang hold their lamas in very high esteem.

If we look more closely into the actual meaning behind this relationship, although it is possible for there to be great affection between friends, it is the master-disciple relationship that seems to have the greatest closeness and affection. Moreover, after the common preliminaries are complete and the uncommon completion stage is received from someone close to us, then the affection between lama and student grows even closer. It cannot be any other way. For example, when students have been led to the natural state of the mind and have actually grasped it, then it is expected that each week the student will offer their realizations to the lama.

Not only this, but from the beginning Jonang monks are introduced to the practice of the six vajra yogas. There is even the custom that one is not truly considered to be a qualified monk unless they have actually developed experiences in the six yogas. When those who are young are found to be unable to have such experiences due to faults in their channels, winds and drops, then they are introduced to physical exercises that allow the experiences to arise more easily. This is one of the things that really impressed me about the Jonang that I had not seen in other lineages. While it cannot be said that these types of experiences can successfully arise in everyone, since the six yogas are practiced continuously, then a continuous relationship of experience and direct instruction is necessarily created between the master and disciple. When it is like this, the desired goal manifests very quickly.

Regarding this way of practicing, the glorious lord Arya Nagarjuna once wrote:

When the guru also meditates,
The student will be blessed.

This teaches that after a completely authentic guru and a student who is a suitable vessel form a relationship by first engaging with the preliminary stages such as studying the texts, then the student's mind is purified and merit is accumulated. Then, by the transference of the guru's blessings, the student's mindstream is ripened by the generation stage and the necessary empowerments. That produces a suitable vessel for developing meditative concentration. Finally, when the guru's blessings are actually united with the student's mindstream, then the fruits of the practice will certainly arise in accordance with the guru's experiential guidance. This is why it is very important and necessary that the oral instructions of the past masters are authentically transferred. Moreover, as Jetsun Taranatha said in the *Ritual for Offering to the Guru*:

Even though one trains in listening, reflecting and meditating
On the sutras and tantras for ten million aeons,
It is taught that without the guru's oral instructions,
The stage of receiving blessings will not be attained.

This also appears in the *Kalachakra Tantra* where it says:

> *Without the oral instructions, confidence does not arise.*

Or as the mahasiddha Ghantapada said:

> *Even though the disc of the sun is very hot,*
> *Without a lens fire will not arise.*
> *Likewise, the blessings of the Buddha*
> *Will not arise without the guru.*

As it is taught there, the guru should also examine closely the mindstream of the student. This necessity to guard the experiential view of the way things are without straying is an unsurpassable quality of the teachings of the Jonang. Otherwise, without the guru's oral instructions and so forth, when one strives in the means of attracting disciples or engages in many dharma activities, then regardless of what happens or whatever is desired, the Dharma will become a cause for guiding others to the lower realms.

In this way, lacking the guru's guidance may become the cause for abandoning the Dharma. When that occurs, from imitating Dharmic actions and aping the external style of gathering students and so forth, there is the danger of being sent directly to the lower realms. Taking the words of the Victorious One as a witness and regarding his explanation as sufficient, we should be very careful to retain this topic in our minds.

* * *

> *The outer guru offers by sending out joy and faith.*
> *The inner guru liberates from the trap of doubt.*
> *The secret guru is self-awareness as buddha-nature.*
> *The guru of suchness is the actual self-awareness.*

16. THE UNIQUE QUALITY OF BEING EXPERIENTIAL DUE TO PRACTICING BOTH SUTRA AND TANTRA WITHOUT CONTRADICTION

As a result of the way that the Buddhist teachings were spread throughout history, the teaching lineages of southeast Asia were mainly drawn from the foundational vehicle. In the eastern traditions of China and so forth, the lineages were mostly drawn from the great vehicle with only a few teachings coming from the cycles of secret mantra which are difficult to grasp. In the himalayan region of central asia both sutra and tantra were established.

In those places where only sutric traditions existed, there was never any attempt to unify the views of sutra and tantra. Even if there was, it was only on a very superficial level. Moreover, after the rise of the view of the ultimate being self-empty became prevalent, there were clear signs that people no longer held the view of mantra to be unsurpassed, complete, infallible and totally correct.

While everyone accepts that tantra is higher than sutra, of those who hold the view of mantra to be unsurpassed there is no one who does not maintain an enlightened mandala, circles of pure deities, mantra and primordial wisdom. If that is the case, then it must also be maintained that those deities of secret mantra are not relative in nature. Newly arisen, relative deities could never embody the inseparable ground and result, great bliss and so forth.

Therefore in accordance with the Jonang explanation of the way things are, the deities are buddha-nature and thus have the primordial nature of inseparable ground and fruition. They are never anything other than this. While these deities of ultimate secret mantra are themselves ultimate and are not empty of their own essences, they are empty of everything other than that—the delusive world of the relative. There is nothing else beyond the ultimate reality—the emptiness of other.

The ultimate profound view of sutra is emptiness. The profound intended meaning of tantra is the non-duality of method and wisdom which is symbolized by the deity Kalachakra and so forth. The unique quality of the Jonang is that they emphasize the union of sutra and tantra just as it is. They make obvious what was not clearly taught by anyone else in the various dharma lineages of the land of snows.

This presentation of the union of sutra and tantra by the Jonang has countless scriptural sources and supportive reasonings. For instance, in the *Perfection of Wisdom Sutra of Seven Hundred Verses* it says:

> ...because the dharmadhatu itself is the Blessed One himself.

Or in the *Sambhuta* where it says:

> Like the light of an immaculate crystal,
> Bodhichitta is luminosity;
> This is the reality
> Of the five primordial wisdoms.

In such words as these, the tantras of secret mantra and the sutras teach in a manner that unifies sutra and tantra. This should be very clear. What is taught by both the sutra vehicle of the perfections and the vajra vehicle of secret mantra is that the luminous space of the dharmadhatu is the great appearance of emptiness. This is taught to be the great inseparable union between great bliss and the five primordial wisdoms.

Among those who know the practices of both sutra and tantra, the realization of this truth cannot be refuted by anyone. However, when sutra and tantra are maintained as separate, then the signs of manifesting this result from practice are quite limited.

As an example of how realization manifests in the Jonang practice, the omniscient Dolpopa says in his *Aspiration for the Two Stages*:

> When primordial wisdom has arrived, grasping of the self ceases...

This is a particular sign that the manifestation of the deities of primordial wisdom have actually arrived. As Dolpopa has also said:

As for the realm of Shambhala, it is manifold.
However, in this land of snows, it is only fully realized in our tradition.

Many other such signs of manifestation are explained in the many texts of the Jonang. As they are rooted in experience, they are difficult to oppose. Furthermore, with regard to what is taught by both the sutras and tantras, their purpose being the same and their presentation as a single pith; the *Lamp of the Three Modes* teaches:

Possessing many means and being without difficulty,
Suitable for those with the sharpest of faculties,
The mantra vehicle is especially exalted.

Then as the great Dzamthang master Lodrö Drakpa taught in his *Roar of Zhentong Madhyamaka from the Fearless One of Five Faces*:

The ultimate way things are in both the sutra and mantra collections is the primordial ground—the dharmadhatu, the singularity of great natural wisdom. That intention is the single substrate for all of reality.

The manner of teaching this in both the sutras and tantras is that successively there is the cause—the empty aspect of the ultimate—and then the result, which is mainly taught as the immutable great bliss aspect of the ultimate. Since specific traditions present these aspects individually, they are taught as the cause and result of the ultimate way things are. Even though in reality they are non-dual and of one taste, for the purposes of teaching they are clearly distinguished.

Regardless of however many or few paths of skillful means may exist, from the perspective of the manner in which they are taught, within the two profound practices of the generation and completion stages that are found within secret mantra, it is extremely clear that the view—both in its scope and its goal—is equivalent with that of the sutras.

However, even though beings of lesser fortune are incapable of knowing this, the excellent sacred mantra whose intention is no different from that of sutra, with its many skilful means, is relatively easy to practice. Since mantra is especially powerful for students with the sharpest of faculties, it is particularly exalted. This realization that the ultimate intended meaning of the sutras and tantras is inseparable as a single pith is one of the unique qualities of the Jonang tradition.

* * *

The highly famed collections of sutra and secret mantra,
If practiced without contradiction teach benefit and happiness.
A state relaxed in freedom from contradiction arises.
If we try to force it, it is doubtful that it will come.

17. THE UNIQUE QUALITY OF UNITY DUE TO KNOWING HOW THE DEITIES, MANTRAS AND MUDRAS ARE JOINED WITH SAMSARA AND NIRVANA

In general, for all qualified lineage holders of the Tibetan traditions, the path is split into two stages—generation and completion. The conceptual meditations used within the generation stage are classified in this way because they generate a state of mind that is in accord with the fundamental way things are. Therefore, what use is there to classify the views of sutra and tantra as being different and saying that there is some other reason?

However, many of those who do claim that sutra and tantra have a single view have still not arrived at a view in which ground and result are inseparable. Regardless of what they claim, if that view of inseparability of ground and result is not embraced, then meditation on the generation stage will definitely not have a manner which accords with how the manifestations of reality are generated.

When one holds this view of the Jonang, then in the beginning, middle

THE EIGHTEEN UNIQUE QUALITIES

and end there is a gradual blossoming which arises in dependence upon the inseparability of ground and result, found in the view of zhentong madhyamaka. Therefore, with conceptuality the main thing that one is striving to produce in the state of generation—that has the nature of emanation and gathering—is not the conceptually labeled deities and so forth.

Even in the generation stage, we are subsumed within the view of the inseparable ground and fruition. The conceptually labelled deities, mantras and mudras—all those with relative reference points—are always pointing towards the assembly of ultimate deities. The reason is because the ground and result are inseparable. The deities, mantras and mudras provide a genuine connection between samsara and nirvana. This is a unique quality of the Jonang tradition. As Dolpopa wrote in his *Clarifying the Meaning of the Dharma*:

As for the uncommon supreme Dharma,
If you understand this, it is also advice.

In relation to this uncommon profound pith instruction, in the *Wish-Fulfilling Jewel of the Middle Way* Taranatha writes:

Furthermore, it is in accord with both ground and result.
Meditating on this is the path of definitive meaning.

As these teachings indicate, if you want to receive the uncommon pith instructions found within the Jonang tradition, they consist of meditating on the union of the generation and completion stages. If you meditate like that, then in reliance upon the essence of all phenomena—buddha-nature—as if by an elixir that transforms iron into gold, the collections of relative phenomena will be transformed into the essence of the five primordial wisdoms and the five or six families of the victorious ones.

In this way, one becomes enlightened in a single lifetime, within a single human body, in as little as a few years or even a few months. Knowing and attaining confidence that we are abiding in the ground of buddhahood, the nature of that ground transforms into the singular nature of mere manifestation.

This does not mean, however, that followers of the Jonang do not or should not meditate on the common generation stage. When "deity, mantra and mudra" are referred to as being held firmly in the mind, the mind is brought closer to the actual deity in a process that has the nature of four limbs—approach, near accomplishment, accomplishment and great accomplishment. When confidence has been attained in viewing reality as the deity, mantra and mudra, then those three will naturally manifest as the deities, mantras and mudras of primordial wisdom during the completion stage. They will manifest fully and completely in all directions like nothing that can be described.

In any case, regarding this completely correct view in which the ground and result are inseparable, Dolpopa wrote in his *Bottomless Ground of the View of Zhentong Madhyamaka*:

> *Those without this base should seriously consider it. It is the very essence of view, meditation and conduct in the sutras and tantras. With the guru's oral instructions for realization, a good attitude and in reliance on good conduct, it will spontaneously arise. In the mind of logicians or in the mind of attachment, it will not arise.*

* * *

> *Like the circle of the sun, it is seen but not seen completely.*
> *Though ground and result appear as the dharmakaya,*
> *they do not appear completely.*
> *Yogins, bodhisattvas and buddhas are levels of realization.*
> *Who doesn't know this?*
> *Happy and carefree in this expanse of ease, logicians need not panic.*

18. THE UNIQUE QUALITY OF BEING INCOMPARABLE DUE TO REACHING THE ULTIMATE MEANING OF THE KING OF TANTRAS, THE GLORIOUS KALACHAKRA

From among the tantras of the later translation period, the glorious Kalachakra is renowned and certainly well established as the King of Tantras. If there are people who think that it is not, then this is merely due to one or more of the three poisons such as attachment, aversion or ignorance. In the Nyingma master Dodrupchen Jigmé Tenpa'i Nyima's *Song of the View* it says:

> *Ati Yoga, the Great Perfection, other than in the manner of being labelled in such a way, is taught to be without higher and lower.*

This is a common statement by many of the learned and accomplished masters of the early translation period. In general, it is quite common that people claim that their personal Dharma tradition is the highest and most profound.

Furthermore, it is clearly evident that those who are and those who are not holders of this Jonang tradition consider the Kalachakra Tantra to be an extremely high and extremely profound teaching unlike any other. Among those who are not holders of our own tradition of Kalachakra, some teach as we do that it is uniquely exalted. However, there are also those who say that while the Kalachakra is very high, the Great Perfection is even higher from the perspective of what is attained. While such individuals may say this, they have no authoritative reasons or evidence with which to back up this claim. Moreover, while some who make such claims may show great enthusiasm in their attitude and strongly maintain this belief, if there are any among them who have clearly established reasons for this assertion, I would ask them to come forward and say what they are.

On the other hand, there are many sets of reasoning—eight, ten, five reasons and so forth—for why the glorious Kalachakra tantra is much more exalted than others. For the sake of brevity I will focus on the set of five here. These are the five wondrous qualities of place, time, retinue, teaching and result which indicate why the Kalachakra is undeniably most exalted:

1. **The wondrous place** in which these teachings arose was within the sambhogakaya realm of the Buddha's meditative absorption.

2. **The wondrous time** was at the juncture of the full moon in the month of Chaitra when there was an ultimate self-arisen appearance of the teacher and disciple as inseparable. All other relative appearances, in which the teacher and retinue manifested as many different individuals gathered together, were simultaneously being taught as the *Perfection of Wisdom Sutras*.

3. **The wondrous retinue** was the Dharma King Suchandra, emanation of the tenth level bodhisattva Vajrapani, along with tens of millions of sages from the northern land of Shambhala.

4. **The wondrous teaching** that was expressed was the profound Primordial Buddha, the king of tantras—glorious Kalachakra—having the three natures of outer, inner and other.

5. **The wondrous result** was that the many tens of millions of sages who were present attained the kayas of union within twelve months.

Possessing this nature as well as many other great qualities, in the minds of those who are to be tamed within the three times the Kalachakra is the most supreme mantric approach. In the past, it is said that the number of those who attained siddhis in reliance on this profound and secret system were more than those who attained siddhis in all of the other systems combined.

Additionally, unlike other systems of tantra, the Kalachakra Tantra

THE EIGHTEEN UNIQUE QUALITIES

contains extensive descriptions of various external and internal sciences such as methods for calculating the positions of planets, detailed descriptions of the subtle energetic system of channels, winds and drops, methods for preparing incenses and balms for the body, and a vast store of Buddhist knowledge. Within this single tantra, all of the vast and profound textual traditions are gathered together without anything being excluded. Then within the chapters dedicated to the "enlightened other," there are extensive teachings on the enlightened mandala and the secret sphere of the dharmadhatu and so forth. There are also a number of very important prophecies describing how a future golden age will arise which are only found in the Kalachakra tantra. In brief, the Kalachakra extensively teaches the exact nature of both samsara and nirvana in the past, present and future. In this way, it is unlike anything found in all of the sutras and tantras of this world. It is for these reasons that it is known as the King of All Tantras.

Furthermore, with respect to the arising of the age of perfection, it is a supreme path without rival that is capable of leading a very wide audience who are ripe to be tamed. Because of its clarity and inclusiveness, it is a direct cause for quickly manifesting the age of perfection, beginning a new cycle of the four ages and establishing the seat of enlightenment. In this time which is close to the auspicious age of perfection, the praises in the vajra scriptures proclaim that this good and wondrous path is undeniably without peer.

For example, in the *Great Commentary on the Root Tantra of Kalachakra* it says:

> *Whoever does not know the excellent Primordial Buddha does not correctly know the Litany of Manjushri's Names. Whoever does not know the Litany of Manjushri's Names does not correctly know Vajradhara's body of primordial wisdom.*

What this means is that within the *Litany of Manjushri's Names*, immutable bliss is identified as essential for the experience of the ultimate. Those who do not realize this teaching fall into the category of samsaric beings. Similarly in the *Abridged Kalachakra Tantra* it says:

> *If someone's mind is purified, that person becomes the lord of the victorious ones, Vajrasattva. What use is there for other victorious ones?*

As it is taught there, it is also taught in other tantras:

> *Individual Withdrawal and Concentration;*
> *Likewise, Life-force Control and Retention;*
> *Recollection and Absorption;*
> *These are the six branches of yoga.*

Through these six branches of yoga, one experiences the three stages of outer, inner and other, the four vajras, the ten signs of luminosity and the four primordial wisdoms of the four joys; thereby one grasps the yoga of the sixteen drops. By means of the primordial wisdom of the twenty-one thousand and six hundred moments of immutable bliss and so forth, one reaches the end of the excellent path of skilful means of the sublime definitive secret—the profound realm of Shambhala.

This is the profound secret of the wheel-turning kings of this world and is the ultimate and innermost natural state that exists within all of the sutras and tantras. On this earth, those who correctly know that this is true and practice accordingly are the practitioners of the glorious Jonang tradition of Dharma. This is the reason why I have expressed all of the above with such great confidence.

* * *

> *Coming from the sublime teachings of Shambhala,*
> *It is the ultimate unification of emptiness and compassion.*
> *May the one that is the King of All Tantras on this earth*
> *Ripen as the auspicious time of the age of perfection.*

CHAPTER FIVE

Clearing Away Faults that Deprecate Zhentong

Having clearly presented the incredibly unique qualities of the Jonang tradition of zhentong madhyamaka, it is now necessary to address specific criticisms of our system in order to remove doubts from the minds of those students who are ripe to establish this view. In the following chapter I will be identifying arguments put forward by many highly respected masters and showing how the Jonang view cannot be defeated by these points.

Please do not misinterpret my motivation for doing this. In general it is extremely difficult to know exactly who is and who is not a holy being. Additionally, for many of the people whom I will mention below, there are many signs in their life stories that indicate that they were indeed holy beings. We can also see that many other beings have been able to rely on their teachings and have achieved extraordinary realizations on that basis. Therefore it is not my place to speak about whether their motivations were virtuous or not. For me as an individual, to the best of my ability I try to maintain a pure view of each of them, holding them in the highest regard and respectfully bowing before them.

However, when my aim is to resolve the differences between the presentation of our views, then it is necessary to address a few very important points. While I won't go into details regarding all of the faults that they claim, I will attempt to clear away the main ones as best I can. When I do this, my criticisms are focused solely on the views, not on the people.

RESPONDING TO SPECIFIC OBJECTIONS FROM GREAT MASTERS

The Fault of the Ultimate Having an Essence

With this in mind, I will begin with Je Tsongkhapa Lobsang Drakpa's *Essence of Explaining the Provisional and Definitive*, where it says:

> With regard to those who say:
>
> > Whatever is taught according to the Perfection of Wisdom and other sutras, that all phenomena are without essence is referring to all relative phenomena, but they are not referring to the ultimate.
>
> > They are saying that if the ultimate was without essence, then that would contradict the commentaries of Asanga and his brother. That would mean that they were outside the tradition of the noble father and sons.

He then goes on to say:

> In particular emptiness, dharmadhatu, suchness and so forth are all stated as different names for the ultimate. Since they are all taught to be essenceless according to these sutras, how could anyone possessing a mind say that the ultimate is not included there?

To answer this claim, I would say that the assertions made in the sutras that phenomena are without essence are understood to be saying that the phenomena of the relative are negated in the actual way things are. Due to there being boundless wrong views, people may still grasp onto the selfhood of a person or phenomena. For those kinds of people there is also the possibility of grasping onto emptiness—dharmata and so forth. In order to negate those, dharma and dharmata are not taught separately. If you then take those teachings literally, it is possible you might think that the dharmata is without essence.

In general, when many proponents of self-emptiness establish the view, they will often not clearly distinguish phenomena and the nature of phenomena—dharma and dharmata. When they do this, it appears that some misconceptions arise. The words of the sutras were taught with the intention to help beings abandon grasping onto relative phenomena. However, in reality there is not one sutra that explicitly says that buddha-nature is essenceless.

The numerous words of the Buddha which taught that the nature of phenomena is truly existent have already been discussed previously. Since the doctrines of Maitreya and Asanga have numerous passages stating this, we do not need to repeat them again here. However, as the noble one Nagarjuna wrote in his *Praise of Dharmadhatu*:

Regarding the sutras that teach emptiness,
As many as were taught by the Victorious One,
By all of them the afflictions are reversed;
But buddha-nature is never harmed by those.

When Asanga, his brother and other learned and accomplished ones teach such words, they are certainly easy to understand. Moreover, although the three kinds of naturelessness are not explained in the same way as in the tradition of Je Tsongkhapa, they are nevertheless well proclaimed in the teachings of the third turning of the Victorious One himself and his spiritual children, as well as in Dolpopa's *Mountain Dharma*, Taranatha's *Ornament of Zhentong Madhyamaka* and many other associated writings. Since those proclamations are supported by scriptures and reasoning, they are firmly established.

If reality were not in the way that the Victorious One and his sons describe, then suchness, buddha-nature, the ultimate truth of cessation and so forth—all those things which are classified as being "ultimate"—would necessarily be non-existent. If that was the case then ultimate truth would not be ultimate. The Dharma of the final turning, its commentaries and the mantras that principally teach that the ultimate truth is the true and reliable reality of primordial wisdom would then necessarily be without an actual referent and would be pointless. No one in their right mind could possibly make such an incredibly consequential statement.

Therefore ultimate truth must necessarily exist, for this is the very definition of what it means for something to be the ultimate way things are. When some say that "it is true, but it does not truly exist" it shows that they are using language in a way that contradicts the basic meaning of the grammar. This is simply a twisting of words in order to establish some sort of unnecessary precision. In addition to making one's statements confusing, it also contradicts the textual tradition of the Victorious One, those of his children and even many ordinary fields of knowledge as well.

I think that it is necessary to actually analyze whether unqualified statements such as "no phenomena truly exist because conventional assertions about them are inconsistent with analysis" are necessary or not for one striving to achieve liberation.

The Fault of Independent Establishment

Then as the excellent Je Tsongkhapa said in his *Provisional and Definitive*:

> *It is maintained that the changeless, perfectly established nature arises as an object of the mind without relying on negation. Such independent establishment is contradictory.*

To this I would answer that when one refers to "objects of the mind", then we should distinguish two types of mind—either conceptual or non-conceptual. When Tsongkhapa says "arising as an object of the mind," he does not clearly distinguish which kind of mind is being referred to. If he is talking about the object of a conceptual mind, then you could not claim that all such conceptual objects rely on negation as you will not find any authentic scripture or reasoning to support that claim. If, however, the object of the mind is specifically referring to a non-affirming negation, then yes, you would need to rely on a negation. However, the Jonang never state that the perfectly established nature is a non-affirming negation so it is impossible for this point to be contradictory.

Furthermore, if it is said that the object is for a non-conceptual mind, then it must fall into one of the four kinds of direct perception. An object that arises in those does not rely on negation. Not only that, just this ultimate truth that is free from elaborations is asserted as an affirming negation.

The highest of noble beings have stated on numerous occasions that affirming negation arising in the mind is primordially established. This means that buddha-nature is not an ordinary affirming negation because it is only recognized by non-conceptual yogic direct perception. That is primordial self-awareness. For this reason it is ultimate establishment. It should not be mistaken with the "establishment" of relative, deceptive truth. This would seem to be a very common mistake. Anyone actually holding such a view should analyze this matter very closely.

The Fault of Being an Incurable View

In speaking about the view that holds the ultimate as being existent, the great scholar Jamyang Shepa's *Commentary on the Provisional and Definitive* says:

> Because father Nagarjuna and his sons explain
> that it is the "incurable view."

My response to this is that he is merely saying that "the protector Nagarjuna said this is an incurable view." This statement however is not supported by any reasoning. It is merely stated as something that Jamyang Shepa wishes to establish. Such an assertion, however, does not in itself establish anything at all. It is merely a statement.

As Dharmakirti wrote in his *Commentary on Valid Cognition*:

> *By stating what is to be established,*
> *The consequences are not proven.*

And also:

> *If there is reasoning for "non-existence,"*
> *At that time it is understood to be non-existent.*

As these passages explain, if you claim to establish something then you have to provide reasons that support your thesis. This is a basic rule of logic in the doctrines of the middle way. However, this noble being did not put forth any reasons for why he thinks that the view of ultimate existence would be an "incurable view". Not only that, but his statement contradicts the statements of Nagarjuna himself and his children who taught, "Nirvana is the only truth." Therefore is it not clear then who is actually teaching outside the tradition of the great pioneers?

If the view taught by the blessed Buddha, his regent Maitreya, Nagarjuna and Asanga is an "incurable view"—implying that everything is self-empty and even the ultimate does not exist—then all of their statements that nirvana is truly existent must be wrong. However, if Nagarjuna, Asanga and Lord Maitreya really proved that the ultimate does not truly exist, then there must be some proof of it in their scriptures. If there is, then I beg all of those who follow Jamyang Shepa to please show it to me so that I may understand.

The Fault of Valid Cognition

Within the textual tradition of the great master of Sera, Jetsun Chokyi Gyaltsen, there is a view that accords with his *Ornament of the Intention of Nagarjuna* which states:

> *The claim that the primordial wisdom of a non-dual grasper and grasped is real and eternal is wrong.*

Those who hold this view then go on to cite a refutation of non-buddhist followers of Shiva that is found in Dharmakirti's *Commentary on Valid Cognition*. There it says:

> *Validly cognized permanence does not exist,*

Because it is valid cognition of real existence.
No excellent teacher has set out
Any proof of such a valid cognition.
Since all knowables are impermanent,
Therefore, it must also be impermanent.

Using this reasoning they try to refute the Jonang view. However, they only refute the valid cognition of the conventional. The permanence of ultimate valid cognition cannot be refuted by any scripture or reasoning. This should be easy to understand by now.

A permanent valid cognition of the conventional is never asserted by the Jonang. This idea does not appear in our doctrine even in the slightest. However, when people try to use the above citation to attack our assertion that buddha-nature and its permanence are validly cognized by primordial wisdom, then this citation simply misses its mark.

In his *Mountain Dharma*, Dolpopa also states that the intended meaning of Dharmakirti's citation is indeed that valid cognition of permanence does not exist. However, the intended scope of that passage is only the valid cognition of relative phenomena, it does not include valid cognition of the absolute. He teaches that all relative knowables are taught as impermanent because they are compounded by temporary conditions.

For such relative phenomena, it is impossible to have faults of contradiction. A third possible classification for these other than real or contradictory is also impossible. Such knowable phenomena must be either real things or unreal non-things. However, ultimate truth is not included within that dichotomy at all.

Those who fling accusations of such a fault close their minds to the point which is actually being taught there. They simply postulate their own opinions as being fundamental truth. Before even understanding what the Jonang are claiming, they are already trying to make assertions to defeat them. This is like trying to say the sun has arisen without ever seeing sunlight.

The Fault of Not According with Dharmakirti

Moreover, even some contemporary scholars try to explain the doctrines of the Jonang and others in accordance with the *Commentary on Valid Cognition*. Since they regard the Jonang view to be exactly the same as the non-buddhist followers of Shiva, they then believe that if one is refuted the other is as well. Likewise if one is established, then the other must also be established. They explain it this way because both the Jonang and the non-buddhists claim that the valid cognition of permanence is ultimate truth. However, they never claim that about the relative.

To such criticisms I would say that when the glorious Dharmakirti says that permanence is refuted and not established as real, he is referring to the valid cognition of conceptual imputations as objects of the mind. Such phenomena can certainly not be established and thus are indeed resolved in accordance with the teachings of Dharmakirti. Since we agree with Dharmakirti, then there is no need to doubt his assertions.

In addition, all of those in India and Tibet who later composed commentaries to his *Commentary on Valid Cognition* resolved that the valid cognition of permanence which is maintained by the non-buddhists must be non-existent in accordance with those teachings.

However, when the Jonang and so forth maintain that buddha-nature is the ultimate way things are, this too is validly cognized. It is not claimed to be permanent out of mere pride in one's own view, nor out of stubbornness. It is the stainless view that was grasped by the blessed Buddha through his own direct experience. Thus it can be proclaimed with certainty.

In Dharmakirti's own writings about the middle way, he says that composers of the sutra tradition did not always make their proclamations in terms of relative valid cognition. This is one of the reasons why he is so highly regarded within the Jonang tradition. Specifically, he has said that the Victorious One, his regent, the two great masters and their children all taught with one intention and one voice. Thus in the *Tathagatagarbha Sutra* it says:

> Like that, I say that all beings are like the example of a gold image covered by clay. The external cover is the husk of the afflictions. Inside it, the primordial wisdom of buddhahood is seen to exist.

And also in the *Great Nirvana Sutra* where it says:

> Son of noble family, what is called "buddha-nature" is the empty ultimate. What is called "the empty ultimate" is also called "primordial wisdom."

Or in the *Sutra of Sublime Golden Light* it says:

> Suchness abides just as genuine primordial wisdom itself. That is the dharmakaya.

And again in the *Samputa Tantra* where it says:

> After completely abandoning all conceptions,
> One abides in the great primordial wisdom that remains.

As well as the *Descent into Lanka Sutra* that says:

> Perfect primordial wisdom, suchness,
> Has the characteristic of complete establishment.

And in the *Litany of Manjushri's Names* it says:

> The kayas of wisdom are self-arising.

In the extensive commentary of *Stainless Light* it says:

> Free from one instant and many,
> Primordial wisdom is the suchness of the victorious ones.

And in the commentary on the root verses of the *Sublime Continuum* it says:

> The undefiled awareness in embodied beings is like honey.

In the *Praise of Dharmadhatu* it says:

> Within the afflictions, primordial wisdom
> Abides as immaculate suchness.

As you can see there is really no end to the scripture and reasoning that establish the view that primordial wisdom abides permanently. Even though the ultimate that is perceived by primordial wisdom is validly cognized, it appears that the idea that primordial wisdom must be impermanent arises due to grasping onto the words in too literal a fashion. I can understand why it happens, but for those who really investigate the meaning closer, that claim is really just meaningless nonsense.

The Fault of Being the Same as non-buddhist Views

Our critics go on to state that the valid cognition which is maintained by non-buddhists possesses the faults which are presented in the *Commentary on Valid Cognition*. Since they think that the Jonang also hold this view, then they must also possess these faults.

To this I would reply that if the valid cognition maintained by non-buddhists actually does contain the same characteristics as that which was taught in the sutras and treatises, then they too should be revered and held up as wonderful! If they teach in accordance with what the Buddha taught, then we see no reason to try to refute them.

In the *Crystal Mirror of Eloquent Explanations*, Lobsang Chokyi Nyima writes:

> *If so, the non-buddhist exponents of Shabda-brahman proclaim that all real things are changes of sound with real natures. The Jonang too appear to assert that the way things are is eternal, stable and pervades all that is animate and inanimate. In particular, very little is not existent for them.*

To answer this I would say that there are no correct or accurate points to be seen by those who try to criticize in this way. Those straightforward scholars who analyze these points in detail will clearly know their lack of accuracy. Furthermore, the view of the non-buddhist proponents of shabda-brahman who proclaim that all real things are changes of sound with real natures are not in the remotest way the same as the view of the Jonang who hold that the ultimate reality pervades all animate and inanimate things.

The proponents of shabda-brahman maintain that the sound OM is the self, the conscious principle or person—that which is known as "purusha." They say that it has nine perceptible characteristics of colour and so forth.

The Jonang maintain that the ground of nirvana—buddha-nature—has many qualities like freedom from elaboration. These defining characteristics are not at all the same. According to the Jonang's proclamation of the great primordial wisdom, the sage—the blessed Buddha—clearly taught in the *Tathagatagarbha Sutra* and others, "I have seen it." The Buddha did not proclaim there that he had a wrong awareness. He proclaimed that he saw that partless all pervading nature, just as it is. Therefore what the Buddha taught is completely different from what the proponents of shabda-brahman taught.

The Faults of Eternalism and Nihilism

In another part of Chokyi Nyima's *Doctrine* he writes:

> *Moreover, in this view postulated by the Jonang the faults of both eternalism and nihilism seem to occur. By proclaiming that the ultimate has a primordially permanent nature they fall into the extreme of eternalism, and then by saying that at the time of relative truth there is existence and then at the time of enlightenment there is non-existence, they fall into the extreme of nihilism.*

To this I respond by saying that the Jonang do not fall into the extreme of eternalism by maintaining that the ultimate truth is permanent. They also do not fall into the extreme of nihilism by maintaining that relative truth is ultimately non-existent. They instead establish their system of the middle way through many scriptural citations and reasonings.

The Jonang view of the ultimate other-emptiness being truly established is held by critics as necessarily meaning that they fall into the extremes of eternalism and nihilism. This fault is not found in the teachings of the Buddha and his children. Simply saying that it "falls into the extremes of eternalism and nihilism" is thus a false accusation.

Moreover, the Jonang never assert that the phenomena of the relative once existed and then later become non-existent. They assert that the phenomena of the relative have primordially never existed at all from beginningless time. As the oral instructions of Dolpopa state:

> *These well known phenomena of the environment and the inhabitants of the three realms are like the horns of a rabbit or a flower in the sky; like the son of a barren woman or butter churned from sand; or like clothing made from tortoise hair. They are primordially non-existent.*

Just as it is taught there, not only are these sights and sounds proclaimed to be non-existent; they are proclaimed in a way that clears away the extremes of eternalism and nihilism. As Jetsun Taranatha wrote in the *Distinction of the Two Modes*:

> *The ultimate other-emptiness is a real thing. It is not newly compounded by causes and conditions. Earlier and later, everything is without change—the permanent stable swastika. Therefore it is not the extreme of nihilism.*

> *It is also not the extreme of eternalism because the ultimate is free from all the extremes of proliferating elaborations. Since it transcends all mentally imputed objects, it cannot be classified by saying "it is like this or that." Thus it transcends the realm of logicians. It is therefore only experienced in self-arisen awareness.*

In accordance with these words and others, the view of the primordial wisdom that is apprehended in the meditations of the noble ones must be presented just as it is. As long as that wisdom is maintained to be without delusion, then the Jonang view will be an accurate presentation of reality that cannot be struck down by faults.

Numerous texts in the glorious tradition of the Jonang teach how to be liberated from the extremes of eternalism and nihilism. The faults that are expressed in the above accusation are completely absent in those texts. Such accusations are without base and pointless as can be seen by simply analyzing them.

The Fault of Not Having Sources

In the *Beautiful Mountain Ornament of the Doctrine that was Taught by the Sage*, Chankya Rolpe Dorje writes:

> *The Jonang view is an incidental view that spreads their own ideas with no learned and accomplished sources at all.*

To this I cannot help but wonder if these words were not in fact some extraneous footnote written by a confused student and not really the words of a learned one like Chankya. However, to respond to this idea I would say that whoever the author is, he was apparently disputing some unfounded stories and had never actually read the teachings of the Jonang masters themselves. If one were to do so, they would see that they are filled with extensive quotes from a wide variety of authentic sources of Dharma.

In any case, what he does not say is that the lineage sources of the Jonang view are among the most respected of all Tibetan Dharma lineages. The authenticity of these texts was clearly explained in texts such as the *Moon Torch of the Jonang History* by Ngawang Lodrö Drakpa from Dzamthang Monastery. Therefore people who hold such a mistaken view should look very closely.

Nowadays people just take it on faith that the Jonang view is heretical and therefore something that should be refuted. If they attempt to do this on the basis of non-realization, wrong realization and so forth, what good could possibly come from it?

Moreover, even though these dharma sources and histories are extensively explained by the Jonang, when prejudiced critics say that the Jonang view is without sources, it may be because they do not explain them in their own tradition. If that was the case, then wouldn't their own tradition also be sourceless because it is not explained in others? This would leave all of Tibet completely destitute of any authentic Dharma.

The Fault of Being the Same as the Samkhya

Chokyi Nyima then goes on to say:

> *Moreover, the way that the Jonang speak about attaining liberation appears not to be different from that of the Hindu Samkhya. The Samkhya include twenty-five categories of knowables.*

And then:

> *The self exists as the knowing awareness of a single person—a purusha—and when nothing else appears, that is maintained as "attainment of liberation."*

And also:

> *Although all relative entities are empty of themselves and hence primordially non-existent, when the ultimate appears to be solitary that is maintained as being the attainment of enlightenment. If this is so, then the two ways of maintaining their views are entirely similar and there is no difference for better or worse between them.*

To this I must respond by saying that the view maintained by the Jonang is not the same as the Samkhya. No unbiased scholar would ever claim otherwise. Except for those who base their claims on prejudice, it has never been the case that they are "entirely similar."

When the Samkhya classify knowables into twenty-five, they use the

CLEARING AWAY FAULTS

following categories: (1) the principal one or nature, *prakriti*; (2) the great, *mahat*; (3) the proud sense of self, *ahamkara*; (4-8) the five subtle elements, *tanmatras*; (9-13) the five gross elements, *mahabhuta*; (14-24) the eleven faculties consisting of five sense organs, *panchendriyas*, five organs of action called *karmendriyas* and the mental faculty of discrimination, reasoning and causitive intelligence known as *manas*; and (25) the self existing as the knowing awareness of a single person, *purusha*.

The twenty-five categories that are used by the Jonang are: (1) the aggregates; (2) the constituents; (3) the sense sources; (4) the nature from which the aggregates arise; (5) the container that is the world; (6) its essence, the forms of sentient beings; (7) the mind; (8) the intellect; (9) consciousness; (10) the phenomena which are the grounds to which characteristics are attributed; (11) the phenomena which are the characteristics that are attributed; (12) unreal phenomena; (13) the ground of feeling; (14) the ground of perception; (15) the ground of formations; (16) the imputation of objects; (17) the imputation of time; (18) the imputation of reality; (19) the unreal things that result from change; (20) the unreal things dependent on real things; (21) those whose existence are impossible; (22) the common path; (23) the uncommon path; (24) the path traveled to the level of a victorious one; and (25) suchness.

The way that these topics are classified is clearly and extensively explained in Taranatha's *Comprehending the Commentaries of the Middle Way of the Great Vehicle*. Other than the mere numbers being the same, it is very easy to see that these two lists are completely different. While the Jonang do indeed use similar numbers and even names as those that are found in Hindu texts, this is a skilful means which has been employed by teachers in order to ripen seeds in students. It is actually a very good thing. If one were to view this as heretical then it is only a sign of ignorance. If all texts that use this technique are condemned as necessarily heretical, then the glorious *Kalachakra Tantra* and a great many others would similarly have to be rejected.

Furthermore, saying that the Jonang lacks any textual tradition for the view that liberation is attained by the relative not appearing and only the ultimate appearing, is so obviously wrong that even saying it refutes itself.

When the relative appears for some minds, the ultimate does not appear. When the ultimate appears for some minds, the relative does not appear. As the regent Maitreya says in his *Distinguishing the Middle and Extremes*:

> *When phenomena appear, the nature of phenomena does not appear.*
> *When phenomena do not appear, the nature of phenomena appears.*

The Jonang view is in accord with that. Too many critics attempt to twist our view to fit with their own misconceptions. Dolpopa and his followers never made such faulty proclamations. If they had, and it was true that positions that are similar in one aspect are necessarily similar in all aspects, then it would be as Taranatha explained in the *Ornament of Zhentong Madhyamaka*:

> *Some even say "because the tradition of other-emptiness is like that of the non-buddhist Samkhya, it is deluded."*
>
> *Even though the cittamatrin view contradicts the non-buddhist traditions, the Treasury of Abdhidharma and so forth, proud of their great and excellent explanations, maintain that the texts of the great vehicle are like those of the non-buddhists. That is crazy talk motivated by harmful envy.*
>
> *If everything that is the same therefore makes it a non-buddhist tradition,*
> *Then the tenets of the four doctrines would all be annihilated.*
> *If being alike in some respects means they are similar in all,*
> *Then the two schools of the shravakas are the same as the Hindu vaisheshikas.*
>
> *The yogacharins would surely be the same as the samkhyas. Being a monk would be the same as being a Jain. Non-buddhist traditions also meditate on compassion. The conduct of secret mantra is similar to that of the shaivites.*

The pancharatra school of Vishnu is similar to the madhyamaka as it also completely transcends mere labelling. Real things and non-things are completely abandoned. They are truly liberated from sending forth and gathering.

King Vaishravana even taught:

> In actuality, reality does not exist.
> Unreality also is without reality.
> Anyone who knows this has insight of suchness,
> And is completely liberated from the real and unreal.

Also it is taught in the Beautiful Composition about Shiva:

> That "the only pure son is supreme" is true.
> He is the lord of insight, with limitless qualities.
> Those who say that he is solitary existence,
> Speak an expression that has an action like a lasso.

According to these words, there are many similarities between teachings of the Hindu doctrines and those of the mahayana. The only exception seems to some extent to be the teachings on self-emptiness. However, to then exaggerate the similarities and say that they are exactly the same would be an incredible fault. In the *Auto-commentary for the Ornament of the Middle Way*, Shantarakshita explains that there are a number of non-buddhist texts which are in accord with Buddhist teachings:

> We have indeed heard about the empty characteristics of Vishnu. We have encountered the great and small songs on the essence, the songs on Shiva and Yuddhisthira, the "sampada" of Shiva and the texts of the samkhyas. The samkhyas have two falsehoods—purusha and prakriti—according with our spoken words. Some of their spoken words also accord with the mantra texts.

> *The texts of Vishnu are like those of the prasangikas. Those of the shaivites sound like those of the svatantrikas. If just two similar aspects make these teachings the same as those who proclaim our own schools, then when the excellent teachings of the samkhyas were heard, us Buddhists would also become these excellent ones.*

What this is saying is that one should not proclaim that Buddhists are outsiders simply because a part of their doctrine is the same as what is taught by outsiders. This should be obvious.

The Fault of Asserting Permanent Defilement

Chokyi Nyima however continues by saying:

> *Such a foundational consciousness, as well as the others which are included within the eight collections of consciousness, have a defiled nature. Saying this is like the non-buddhist analysis of their assertions about the nature of a defiled mind.*

To this I would then say that for an outsider's analysis, defilement and mind exist in a mixed state, and it is not possible to abandon them or be separate from them. The Jonang however, like all Buddhists, claim that the eight collections of consciousness are not inseparably mixed with afflictive states of mind and other defilements, and therefore it is certainly possible to separate them. This enlightened mind does not accord with the relative mind that Chokyi Nyima is teaching. Such a mind has a primordial luminous nature. It has never actually been covered by defilments. This is like it is said in Nagarjuna's *Praise of Dharmadhatu*:

> *Within the afflictive states of mind,*
> *Primordial wisdom abides without stains just like that.*

In the same way, what is taught by the Jonang is valid cognition of ultimate truth. The relative valid cognition, which is thought to refute it, never arises for the mind of a Jonang practitioner. Therefore such a mind can never authentically refute the Jonang view.

On the contrary, this view is fully established. As Dharmakirti wrote in his *Commentary on Valid Cognition*:

Because of being permanent and without extremes,
How could the methods not also be known?

This teaches that one should abandon notions like those of the Hindus that claim stains to be permanent and without extremes. Since the Jonang never proclaim this, why do these critics persist in saying they do?

The Fault of Not According with Nagarjuna

While it is believed that Gowo Rabjampa once mentioned that Jetsun Remdawa made accusations but failed to give details about what they were, and since I feel that I have refuted this many times before, I don't think we need to spend too much time on this.

However to illustrate some of these criticisms, there is the idea that proponents of other-emptiness are somehow "outside" of the tradition of Arya Nagarjuna and that there are no words which establish this idea within Nagarjuna's *Collection of Reasoning* nor his *Collection of Praises*. The fact that there are indeed words which establish the view of other-emptiness in the beginning, middle and end of those texts is well established and so that fault need not be addressed here.

If you absolutely must have an example, then we can see in the *Praise of Dharmadhatu* where Nagarjuna says:

From among the sutras teaching emptiness
That were taught by the Victorious One,
By all of these the afflictions are reversed.
But buddha-nature is not harmed.

Just as water abiding within the earth
Is without defilements.
So too, the primordial wisdom abiding in the afflictions
Is without defilements.

Such words are seen in many places and there is no reasonable reason to argue against them. For instance, in the *Sublime Continuum* it says:

> That which has the characteristics of being separable
> Is pure of the adventitious; therefore its nature is empty.
> However, that which has the characteristic of being inseparable
> Is the unsurpassable Dharma; therefore it is not empty.

Also the Manjushri's *Brief Teaching Establishing the View* says:

> The emptiness that comes from analysing the aggregates
> Is like a plantain tree that has a core.
> The emptiness that possesses all supreme aspects
> Is not like that.

These passages teach in accordance with the many other passages found in the textual traditions of Maitreya and Manjushri, or Asanga and Nagarjuna. This is easy to verify. Specifically, however, the foundation of the Jonang view of other-emptiness is laid out in the texts of the exalted Maitreya and Asanga. The texts of the noble Nagarjuna say that there is certainly no way of refuting perception; only the existence of the eight extremes that are subsequently projected onto that. The only exception is when faulty assertions are imputed. Those indeed can be refuted.

Even though a lesser being such as myself cannot understand the criticisms of the excellent scholar of the Sakya school, who is surely an emanation of the buddhas and bodhisattvas, I can still gain confidence by knowing that I have many citations and a pure motivation to seek reality just as it is. From what I see in the teachings, the validity of pure perception is vividly clear and the mistaken aspect is clearly explained. If realized beings can verify that Remdawa's criticisms of the Jonang are true, then perhaps there is great benefit for them to come forward and help myself and those like me. Therefore, to those beings I humbly request that you present your excellent explanations which have yet to exist.

OTHER COMMON MISCONCEPTIONS

If I were to attempt to answer every one of the baseless criticisms that people raise, there would be a great host of words that don't really seem to be necessary. Therefore, instead I would like to offer a short summary of the most common misconceptions that should clear away various faults in one fell swoop.

I would like to start by looking at the commentarial style of many present day proponents of other-emptiness who seem to have confusion in relation to what "freedom from elaborations" actually means. As Dolpopa Sherab Gyaltsen said in his *Mountain Dharma*:

> *In accordance with the middle turning, after meditating on the transcendently profound nature of phenomena as non-conceptual and free from elaboration, then during the clear distinctions of post meditation, when phenomena are correctly discriminated individually, that is similar to what is taught in the final turning and also in the vajrayana. If that is pointed out with good distinctions...*

Some who comment on this passage say that when the ultimate way things are is reached, it is buddha-nature free from elaborations. They claim that this view has no difference at all from the proponents of self-emptiness and is drawn from the same scriptural sources.

However, others say that it is not really like that and by quoting scriptures they claim that the meditation of the noble ones is a non-perception free from elaborations that is essentially the absence of experiencing anything at all. However, such commentaries also say that no one has arisen to clarify whether this is or is not the way things actually are. This shows that they do not understand the meaning of the above quote.

While I agree that the ultimate way of all phenomena is the buddha-nature free from all elaborations, if one fixates too strongly onto the idea of "freedom from elaborations", then that is a grave error because buddha-nature is filled with the countless ultimate elaborations of the dharmakaya. To say that those qualities are not experienced by the primordial wisdom of a noble one's meditation is a great and irreversible fault because it asserts that what is apprehended by the primordial wisdom of a noble one's meditation does not correspond to reality.

The intended meaning of the scripture being discussed is that when yogins meditate, at the time of experiencing the primordial wisdom of a noble one's meditation, then all of the elaborate characteristics of the relative must be transcended. This could never mean that the primordial wisdom of a noble one's meditation merely experiences a freedom from any sort of elaboration.

When it says "during the clear distinctions" as described above and in reliance on Dolpopa's own annotations, it is clear that one must completely let go of those relative elaborations. However, we must not forget the use of the verb here. If one does not understand the subtle meaning of the verb "meditate" in "after meditating on the transcendently profound nature of phenomena as non-conceptual and free from elaboration," then one will clearly not penetrate into the deeper meaning.

If you analyze this statement with reasoning, the profound nature of phenomena—buddha-nature—will be understood. In such an understanding, it should be obvious that all elaborations of relative conceptual characteristics are separated. I think everyone can agree on that.

The reason is because whatever actions that are done with a conceptual mind are necessarily done with elaborations. It cannot operate without elaborations. Therefore in order to go beyond the elaborations of relative truth, one must rely on non-conceptual primordial wisdom. Otherwise it is impossible to experience buddha-nature.

The manner of negating the elaborations is in reliance on the authentic doctrines of the buddhas, especially the pith instructions of the lamas. On the basis of those, one must negate all conceptions. Otherwise there will be no way for a non-conceptual mind that is completely free from conceptual elaborations to arise without perpetually turning the wheel of the conceptual mind.

However, the essence of what is being said here is that many people have these misconceptions and lack understanding because they hear the words "the primordial wisdom of a noble one's meditation must be free from all elaborations" and they do not understand that it is talking about how to meditate. Instead they think that these instructions are descriptions of how buddha-nature actually exists.

Commentaries that say that no elaborations of any kind can exist in buddha-nature are simply wrong. Such authors may think that they are presenting a view of the way things are from the perspective of other-emptiness, but in the end they are simply holding that buddha-nature is empty of itself. How could the truth of the way things are be non-existence? Suchness, the buddha-nature that is empty of other, is also characterized as necessarily having the nature of countless ultimate elaborations. Its being characterized in that way is not dependent on its being free from the characteristics of the relative which are the objects of refutation, nor on there being someone who classifies how the mind of meditation is free from elaboration. The ultimate buddha-nature primordially has the nature of limitless ultimate qualities.

To this you might think, "Saying that is just wrong and is not taught by any of the learned and accomplished ones of India or Tibet." Then I would say that you are free to make that statement, but it then follows that freedom from elaboration is not a non-conceptual primordial wisdom, because I am saying that it is not actually free from elaborations.

When such authors speak of "the elaborations of the ultimate," they often leave out the word "ultimate" and therefore, when the idea of elaborations is asserted, they respond by saying that this means buddha-nature must be completely free from elaborations. Just that is enough to establish a wrong view and produce many forms of attachment to literal words, such as grasping onto the words "freedom from elaboration" and so forth. This is a clear sign that they have not actually realized the non-conceptual ultimate way things are.

Also, if they are advocating for freedom from elaborations simply in order to win an argument, then due to the faulty motivations of the eight worldly dharmas, their teachings are completely absent of any profound beneficial points. Some, even though they lack such faulty motivation, are so accustomed to the habit of saying "freedom from elaborations" and to not allowing for any "elaborations" whatsoever, that they hold tightly to those habits without even thinking. While they are convinced that they are accurately describing the way things are, there is simply no validity in their statements.

The reason for this is that they do not take other interpretations into account. This leads them to misunderstand the fundamental meaning of these teachings and to cling to the view that they are most familiar with. However, when the mind is left naturally, they may think that they need to persistently attempt to destroy all appearances.

A sensible person, however, should be able to recognize that all elaborations need not be bad. Rather than thinking that all elaborations are definitely wrong, it makes much more sense to establish good and bad elaborations based on clearly distinguishing the kind of ground that is being elaborated upon and in what way the elaborations are arising. Knowing this, one is able to discriminate which kinds of elaborations should or should not be separated from which kind of ground.

For example, at the time of luminosity there are certainly also some elaborations. In that, one is certainly relaxed and blissful. Since all the distinctive qualities of the ultimate reality are its elaborations, then it does not need to be separated from them. If one can understand that such separation is neither desirable nor possible, then from that point forward, one's mind becomes relaxed and blissful.

At the time of meditating on the way things are, in the beginning a yogin must meditate with a mind that is entirely free of phenomena. Then the buddha-nature whose nature is the arising of all aspects will be experienced. Otherwise, if one starts to meditate with a mind that is filled with conceptual characteristics, then the buddha-nature which is endowed with the nature of the countless qualities of the dharmakaya cannot be grasped. It can only be realized through the experience of self-aware primordial wisdom.

Within this tradition, actual non-conceptual mind is not achievable through the analysis of conceptual mind because conceptual mind looks outward upon dualistic appearances of subject and object. However, suchness or buddha-nature is not like that. Buddha-nature is necessarily separate from all dualistic elaborations of the relative.

Saying that nothing should be experienced from within a noble one's meditation on buddha-nature other than a mere freedom from elaborations is utter nonsense. Those who assert this are clearly not paying attention to the most basic rules for logic and meaning.

Based on Dolpopa's own notes for the *Mountain Dharma*, if I were to add comments into the above passage, I would say:

(When one practices by completely abandoning conceptual thoughts) in accordance with the middle turning, after meditating on the transcendently profound nature of phenomena as non-conceptual and free from elaboration (which is like been roused from deep sleep into a dream),

The meaning of saying "by completely abandoning conceptual thoughts" should be easy to understand. The words "meditating on" are also clear. Then later it says:

then during the clear distinctions of post meditation (which is like fully waking from sleep), when phenomena are correctly discriminated individually, that is similar to what is taught in the final turning and also in the vajrayana. If that is pointed out with good distinctions, within the context of the complete practice of the profound meaning that is found within the scriptures of the Mahayana, then one will not make mistakes and will be completely correct.

What this is saying is that if this kind of meditation is performed, in this way that accords with reality, there is existence and nonexistence, being empty and not empty of itself, faults that are relinquished and virtues that are accepted, non-affirming negation and affirming negation, abandoning and realizing, and so forth. Discriminating well how they all abide within the nature of phenomena is what is being taught.

Thus, by these words and those that follow, it is very clear that buddha-nature is not a mere freedom from elaborations, because it possesses all enlightened qualities. Therefore it is futile to try to establish an unproven, apparent thesis which refutes reality. Such an act is simply a waste of the precious freedoms and endowments of this human birth. We should take care to avoid that at all costs.

From practicing other meditations that focus on relative truths generated by the mind, one tries to explain that as being sufficient to realize ultimate truth. However, suchness can never be a reality of mere freedom from elaborations in the sense of them being a mere absence. If it were, then the claim that the ultimate is endowed with all aspects, has all enlightened qualities, has the nature of countless immaculate qualities and so forth—all of these many classifications would be destroyed.

Some critics may then say that the idea of the ultimate being endowed with all qualities is merely a provisional classification of the relative mind in post meditation. Relying solely on the practice of the middle turning, they maintain that ultimate truth which is without faults of contradiction and incongruity is nothing more than a featureless freedom from elaboration. This is a great deprecation of reality and should be considered a major trap for the mind.

From the immaculate Dharma of our blessed Teacher in the many sutras and tantras that have been preserved in Tibet, it is very clear that the great middle way of other-emptiness correctly teaches the ultimate way things are. This is established clearly by a great many scriptures and valid reasonings. There is nothing in the scriptures which can be seen to contradict it. Similarly, it should be just as clear that the view of self-emptiness is not the ultimate.

The only reason that we are not able to achieve enlightenment in this life is due only to the presence of powerful habitual propensities; to being fixated on one's own personal views; or to spending all of one's time perpetuating specific biased arguments. Even if all of these are true, there is still hope for liberation because we can let go of holding our biases as supreme from this moment forward. The way to do this is through the paths of seeing and habituation. This accords with the appearance of the higher perceptions.

While translations of the various scriptures have been arranged to help you clear away your doubts, it is important that we do not distort them to suit our own personal preferences. They are excellent explanations just as they are and should be preserved as authentically as possible. In the end, however, it is my sincere hope that through this clear language, your mind may be liberated from misconceptions.

— *Jetsun Taranatha* —
Unbiased master of the Six Vajra Yogas of Kalachakra.

CHAPTER SIX

Excerpts from the Textual Tradition

Regardless of how much you agree with my motivation, there is still value in making this analysis, even if it is just to help me overcome my own dispositions for laziness. Without any innate rhetorical skill, I have made this explanation with the hope that it will be of some small benefit, helping you to identify the important key points that are generally hard to verify.

Now as a final summary of this work, I would like to offer translations of the actual words of the two great Tibetan masters who completely clarified the definitive meaning—Dolpopa Sherab Gyaltsen and Jetsun Taranatha.

EXCERPT FROM "THE LUMINOUS UNION" BY JETSUN TARANATHA

The first excerpt that I have chosen comes from the Luminous Union that was written by Jetsun Taranatha. In this text, the view of other-emptiness—the great middle way of the age of perfection—is shown to completely uproot all grasping onto selfhood and characteristics. Here with its especially esteemed manner, the ultimate view—like an indestructible thunderbolt—is explained in relation to the profound path of vajra yoga and is very useful for dispelling objections that fall outside this view due to being written in the manner of responses to questions. When I first read it, I developed a deep aspiration that all beings might realize this ultimate truth and therefore I have included it here.

The vajra yoga is the yoga of the ultimate great middle way, that which unites referential emptiness with the non-referential compassion of immutable bliss. The three occasions of ground, path and fruition arise because they all abide within this ultimate middle way. Thus the king of tantras, the glorious *Kalachakra*, says:

> *As for damaging the thesis of one who is an exponent of non-dual emptiness and compassion, it cannot be damaged.*

Also in the *Great Commentary*, with regard to such emptiness and compassion, it says:

> *The compassion that is present here is non-referential and the emptiness that is free from conceptual thoughts is endowed with all supreme aspects. For the sake of knowing the three times, one enters into the three times.*

To this some may object by saying, "Isn't it taught that the middle way is the way things are beyond extremes?" Such as in:

> *Non existent, not non-existent and not both,*
> *And also not of the nature of neither,*
> *Completely liberated from the four extremes,*
> *Just this is encountered by the practitioners of the middle way.*

Doesn't this say that in both conventional descriptions and experiential realization of the way things are, that the middle way is freedom from extremes? Likewise, when the scriptures say:

> *Thus when all apparent phenomena*
> *Are sought by reasoning, none are found.*
> *Their not being found is the ultimate.*

Is this not true? By a thorough analysis of knowable objects, they are grasped as primordially never having existed. When we are involved with the appearance of objects, grasping the mind just abiding in itself is classified, merely conventionally, as realizing freedom from extremes.

In brief there is nothing to realize, because in the absolute nothing is established at all. As this relative is mere empty appearance, it is not said that it is existent or non-existent, nor that it is or is not. This assertion is the proper understanding of the middle way of ground, path and result. However, bliss does exist to be experienced and illusion-like reflections exist as something to be seen. These real things exist conventionally as phenomena of the relative.

To this I would reply, just this is not proper reasoning of the middle way. Suchness as you describe it would be an aspect that is completely cut off. It would not be the abiding mode which is similar to the union that establishes complete enjoyment. Also by meditating on such an ultimate, grasping at real things is not reversed because the existence of real things has the contradiction of grasper and grasped. As the saying goes, "By ascertaining that a tree exists in the east, the ascertainment of a mountain existing in the west is not reversed."

Like this, by such reasoning, those logicians who are arrogant about having realized the nature of phenomena turn their backs on the ultimate mode of abiding of the definitive meaning. As a result they cannot assimilate the profound secret mantra with such a great darkness of wrong conception.

While these logicians have certainly analyzed the two truths in a very extensive way, if we penetrate down to the essence it is like this: in worldly opinion, if there is a certainty that a lion is in a particular cave, we can realize that no fox will be there. If it is certain that the sun has arisen, we can realize that darkness is absent. Similarly, if it is certain that the ultimate primordial wisdom exists primordially within the three realms, then we can realize that the three realms of relative consciousness have never existed from the very beginning.

By meditating on the bliss and empty form, grasping to real things and the appearance of real things are both reversed. The union of empty form and immutable bliss transcends the extremes of negation and establishment, real and unreal, existence and non-existence, being and non-being. That is because it is the unconditioned, uncompounded ultimate.

The establishment of substantial things is certainly not independent, but even without reasoning, if you say it is "substantial" then you are forcefully superimposing upon them various extreme forms of bias and absurd consequences. However, what use is there to respond to the mere freedom from extremes in your tradition? Whether superimposed on real or unreal things, without a reason, they are the same.

At the time of the path, even though the meditative absorption of blissful peace and diligence is a real thing and compounded, it is also the means for reversing the grasping onto real things, like the fire that arises from wood and burns away both itself and the wood.

For this reason the primordial wisdom that is free from all extremes is what is realized by yogins. This is what is attained by those who meditate on the path, is what is known by the buddhas and is suitable to be the abiding mode which enters into all phenomena. However, the mere freedom from extremes that you maintain is none of those. It cannot be established as the suchness that is realized, attained, known or abided in. Rather, it is completely unsuitable for being realized, attained, known or abided in.

If suchness does not exist, then the awareness that realizes it does not exist either; therefore the liberation of that awareness is impossible. If liberation can exist separately from realization by awareness, then everyone would be equally liberated and non-liberation would be impossible. Thus attainment, realization and so forth would be non-existent. If you think that you will be liberated by simply knowing that they are non-existent, that is also impossible because you—the knower—are non-existent as well.

Therefore even though it is taught that phenomena are completely non-existent in order to cut attachment to substantial things, from the perspective of the noble ones the nature of phenomena and what is realized by primordial wisdom is not like that. If one asks what is the Dharmadhatu like in the individual and personal awareness of a noble one, it is co-emergent primordial wisdom. For an example, think of how poison can be removed from good food so that it can be tasted and eaten; however, if poison is recognized to be non-existent, that doesn't help you to eat eternally non-existent food.

The experienced perceptions of immutable bliss and empty form are never perceived by the eight collections of consciousness, but they are experienced by the self-aware primordial wisdom which knows itself. As it says in the *Brief Teaching Establishing the View*:

> *The emptiness that comes from analyzing the aggregates*
> *Like a plantain tree, is without a heart.*
> *The emptiness having all supreme aspects*
> *Is not like that.*
>
> *Being without arising and without cessation,*
> *All knowables are perceived in just this way.*
> *The entity of being empty is emptiness.*
> *It is not the vacuity of analyzing the aggregates.*

Just as it is taught there, when the emptiness of mere freedom from extremes is made into the object of a mind's habitual way of grasping, meditation does not transcend the conceptual, because such an unreal object can never be made the object of a non-conceptual awareness. It can never be the kind of emptiness that must be meditated on. It can only be understood by hearing and contemplation.

SUPPLICATIONS TO THE DEFINITIVE MEANING
BY DOLPOPA SHERAB GYALTSEN

The second excerpt is a short prayer of supplication by the omniscient one Dolpopa Sherab Gyaltsen titled Supplications to the Definitive Meaning. Through reading this prayer, I hope you will establish the necessary connections to actualize the profound view in your mind.

OM. I supplicate the guru and three jewels.
Please grant us your blessings!

How pitiful are those who mistake consciousness and primordial wisdom as one. Please hold us with compassion!

How pitiful are those who mistake self-emptiness and other-emptiness as one. Please hold us with compassion!

How pitiful are those who mistake the relative and the ultimate as one. Please hold us with compassion!

How pitiful are those who mistake phenomena and the nature of phenomena as one. Please hold us with compassion!

How pitiful are those who mistake the extremes and the middle as one. Please hold us with compassion!

How pitiful are those who mistake the fabricated and the natural as one. Please hold us with compassion!

How pitiful are those who mistake the incidental and the fundamental as one. Please hold us with compassion!

How pitiful are those who mistake the imputed and the thoroughly established as one. Please hold us with compassion!

How pitiful are those who mistake the afflictions and complete enlightenment as one. Please hold us with compassion!

How pitiful are those who mistake samsara and nirvana as one. Please hold us with compassion!

How pitiful are those who mistake the truths of suffering, origination and cessation as one. Please hold us with compassion!

How pitiful are those who mistake the outer, inner and the supreme other as one. Please hold us with compassion!

How pitiful are those who mistake faults and enlightened qualities as one. Please hold us with compassion!

How pitiful are those who mistake the exhaustible and the inexhaustible as one. Please hold us with compassion!

How pitiful are those who mistake the defiled and the undefiled as one. Please hold us with compassion!

How pitiful are those who mistake the bad and the good as one. Please hold us with compassion!

How pitiful are those who mistake the born and the unborn as one. Please hold us with compassion!

How pitiful are those who mistake the made and the unmade as one. Please hold us with compassion!

How pitiful are those who mistake the arising and the non-arising as one. Please hold us with compassion!

How pitiful are those who mistake destruction and non-destruction as one. Please hold us with compassion!

How pitiful are those who mistake movement and non-movement as one. Please hold us with compassion!

How pitiful are those who mistake the conceptual and the non-conceptual as one. Please hold us with compassion!

How pitiful are those who mistake consciousness and buddhahood as one. Please hold us with compassion!

How pitiful are those who mistake sentient beings and buddhas as one. Please hold us with compassion!

How pitiful are those who mistake discursive thoughts and the dharmakaya as one. Please hold us with compassion!

How pitiful are those who mistake the husk and the core as one. Please hold us with compassion!

How pitiful are those who mistake falsehood and truth as one. Please hold us with compassion!

How pitiful are those who mistake deception and non-deception as one. Please hold us with compassion!

How pitiful are those who mistake non-existence and existence as one. Please hold us with compassion!

How pitiful are those who mistake illusion and non-illusion as one. Please hold us with compassion!

How pitiful are those who mistake suffering and bliss as one. Please hold us with compassion!

How pitiful are those who mistake karmic forms and luminosity as one. Please hold us with compassion!

How pitiful are those who mistake what is to be abandoned and what is to be accepted as one. Please hold us with compassion!

How pitiful are those who mistake what is to be rejected and what is to be attained as one. Please hold us with compassion!

How pitiful are those who mistake what is to be purified and the ground of purification as one. Please hold us with compassion!

How pitiful are those who mistake the produced result and the separated result as one. Please hold us with compassion!

How pitiful are those who mistake the producer and the separator as one. Please hold us with compassion!

How pitiful are those who mistake the five poisons and primordial wisdom as one. Please hold us with compassion!

How pitiful are those who mistake poison and nectar as one. Please hold us with compassion!

How pitiful are those who mistake darkness and light as one. Please hold us with compassion!

How pitiful are those who mistake enemies and friends as one. Please hold us with compassion!

How pitiful are those who mistake distinctions and transcendence as one. Please hold us with compassion!

How pitiful are those who mistake meditation and post-meditation as one. Please hold us with compassion!

How pitiful are those who have many mistaken traditions due to many mistaken foundations. Please hold us with compassion!

How pitiful are those who—having met with the Dharma of the age of perfection—have come under the power of the Dharma of those with the faults of the age of three parts and below. Please hold us with compassion!

How pitiful are those who while grasping onto that as being not that, under the great influence of previous slander, deceive all sentient beings. Please hold us with compassion!

Fathers, mothers and children, in a flaming pit of suffering,
How unbearable it is to see them fall!
Like that, this supreme supplication has arisen
From the power of unbearable compassion.

THE GREAT MIDDLE WAY

While some may hate me,
I am always free from hatred.
There is only fear of transgression
And joy when there is good.

To tell the reason for this,
While transgressing ethical discipline is easy,
The view should never be harmed.
These words are for the sake of extensively teaching that.

Oh my! Oh my! This degenerate age!
In particular, the degeneration of view is rampant.
Therefore there is much damage to the view,
And transgressions of conduct abound.

When the compassionate noble ones fully see
The damage that is being done to both,
With correct view, meditation and conduct,
May they bring their complete and perfect blessing.

This supplication of the ultimate definitive meaning is called the "superior supplication." It was composed by the vagabond having the four reliances. By this may there be benefit for the teachings and for sentient beings. Auspiciousness!

Conclusion

By this merit, may the host of incidental defilements
Co-emergent with the life-supporting and downward-voiding winds,
In reliance on the profound methods with all their gentle power,
May we quickly attain buddha-nature, the supreme other.

Whatever white virtues there may be from striving like this,
May the ocean of aspirations mix with the excellent assembly
Of the bodhisattvas such as the Kalki Kings of Shambhala.
May the second golden age of this world manifest.

In the exalted mind that is free from contamination, there is no delusion.
Under the power of the compassion of the bodhisattvas of the great bhumis,
After immediately establishing all the objects of aspiration,
May we enter into this excellent path of primordial connection.

Stretching over the span of many thousands of years,
Hundreds of thousands of great ones expounded their view and doctrine,
With finely detailed presentations that logically establish discriminating wisdom.
Therefore this analysis may be seen by some as shameful.

However, I did not write this text out of arrogance or a desire to show off,
Nor to elicit praise for myself out of attachment.
My main concern was to expose anything I did not know or didn't realize
Within my own propensities for the Tibetan Dharma.

If there is any good that comes from this text, it is as a result
Of the kindness of many holy masters, texts and dharma friends.
Therefore without any conditions for arrogance to arise,
I dedicate any good virtues so that it may bring benefit and
happiness to others.

Whatever aspects of error or confusion that may exist here,
They are only my own and I sincerely apologize and regret them.
If there are those who sincerely criticize my efforts here,
Then may I hold them as my most precious Dharma friends.
May I not respond negatively to those who speak with attachment and aversion

Without the fame of being a great scholar, and without the external signs of accomplishment, having some intuition for how to distinguish self-emptiness and other-emptiness, I, an unknown wanderer who cycles quietly, strove to make this subject easier to understand by writing this text.

Even though I made no effort to make the writing poetic, and even though I lack the capacity to fully explain its profundity, if there are any suitable words that fit with these times, then I dedicate any merit to the realization of the view of the age of perfection.

With an intuition for the profound propensities of this Dharma of the age of perfection, From this act may I aspire to only serve the Dharma of the age of perfection. In accordance with this complete age of perfection, may perfect bliss and happiness arise and transform this world into a new golden age.

COLOPHON

The sources for this work can all be traced back to the texts of the Omniscient One Possessing the Four Reliances, the Buddha from Dolpo and the beautiful adornments which were written by Jetsun Taranatha. Born in the southern part of the Golok region, I am the one who is known by some in the east and west as Shar Khentrul Rinpoché, or by my Dharma name Jamphel Lodrö. I wrote this text in the seventeenth year of the current sixty-year cycle, the earth dog year in the Tibetan calendar of 992 (2018), on the second day of the Nagpa month. Without intending it to be this way, the text was completed amidst the auspicious signs which naturally arose in the Chinese city of Shanghai. It was written so that all those who encountered it might realize and practice the view of the essence of the definitive meaning and so that a new golden age of global peace and harmony might quickly be established. May this be a cause for everyone to live in accord with the glory of peace and harmony.

This text was translated from Tibetan into English by Ives Waldo in 2018 and then lightly edited by Ven. Tenpa'i Gyaltsen in 2019.

— *Khentrul Rinpoché Jamphel Lodrö* —

About the Author

Khentrul Rinpoche is a nonsectarian master of Tibetan Buddhism. He has devoted his life to a wide variety of spiritual practices, studying with more than twenty-five masters from all of the major Tibetan traditions. While he has genuine respect and appreciation for all spiritual systems, he has the greatest confidence and experience with his personal path of the Kalachakra tantra as taught in the Jonang-Shambhala tradition.

Rinpoche brings a sharp and inquisitive mind to everything he does. His teachings are accessible and direct, often emphasizing a very pragmatic sensibility. Over the years, Rinpoche has authored a variety of books to guide his students and has specifically made great efforts to translate and provide commentary on texts that present the gradual stages of the Kalachakra path.

Rinpoche has no doubt that our world has the potential to develop genuine peace and harmony, while still preserving its environment and humanity. He believes this golden age of Shambhala is possible through the study and practice of the Kalachakra system. To this end, Rinpoche travels the world to share his knowledge of this unique lineage, free from sectarian bias.

Recognizing that lasting genuine happiness is only possible through profound personal transformation, Khentrul Rinpoche's main focus is to introduce the world to the unique path of the Kalachakra tantra. Up until now, the complete teachings of this tradition have remained in Tibet where they have been preserved by the Jonang tradition of Tibetan Buddhism.

It is Rinpoche's life mission to bring this wisdom into the world at a time when it is so desperately needed. There are four ways in which Rinpoche accomplishes this goal.

Teaching the Essence of the Kalachakra Tantra

The Kalachakra Tantra is known as the king of tantra due to its profound wisdom regarding the nature of reality and its vast quantity of skillful methods for actualizing that wisdom in one's own experience. When compared with other tantras, the Kalachakra system can appear extremely complex and overwhelming to all but the most astute of practitioners. For this reason, Khentrul Rinpoche invests a great deal of his time and energy toward communicating the essential meaning behind the teachings so that students at any level of development can approach and draw benefit from this system.

To this end, Rinpoche travels around the world introducing students to five main subjects that can be used to understand the various aspects of Kalachakra practice: (1) understanding the relationship between Shambhala and Kalachakra, (2) how to remove bias through a nonsectarian philosophy, (3) how to identify the definitive meaning through the view of other-emptiness, (4) how to practice the common and uncommon preliminaries of Kalachakra, and (5) how to practice the six vajra yogas of the Kalachakra completion stage.

Preserving the Lineage through Writing and Translating

To support an ever-expanding community of Kalachakra practitioners, Rinpoche recognizes the need to have quality materials for both study and practice. By relying on his various books, students can build on the teachings they receive and, thereby, prepare themselves for future practices.

While Rinpoche's oral teachings emphasize the essence of Kalachakra, Rinpoche's books present the path in great detail, providing a clear structure for working through the vast material in a gradual manner.

In addition to his original works, Rinpoche also collaborates with translators in order to communicate to the world the ancient wisdom of the Kalachakra lineage masters. His aspiration is to make the Kalachakra teachings available in every major language, reducing the barriers to study and practice for international students.

Creating a Global Community of Kalachakra Practitioners

The golden age will not occur as a result of a single event but as a cumulative result of the combined efforts of the people on this planet. We, as individuals, first need to learn to cultivate peace and harmony within our own minds in order for it to arise in our world. Understanding this, Rinpoche actively encourages his students to build spiritual communities that promote the cultivation of qualities such as love, compassion, and wisdom. Through their shared practice of Kalachakra, these communities will form a global network of practitioners, dedicated to the actualization of their enlightened nature.

Rinpoche achieves this by working closely with his students, generating abundant opportunities for them to accumulate merit and for them to strengthen the karmic connection with each other. He does this mainly through encouraging his students to participate in the many varied Dharma related projects he oversees and coordinates. These projects range from simple administrative tasks to more complex ventures such as building ornate holy objects. It also includes organizing international tours and events where communities can come together and bond as a single vajra family.

Building Retreat Centers for Intensive Practice

The last component for actualizing the golden age is to create the physical infrastructure required to support long-term retreat in conditions conducive to meditation. Not only is it necessary to have locations where students can dedicate themselves to the teachings, it is also important to create connections with yogic practitioners who can guide students through the various experiences that arise during advanced retreat.

At this time, the most extraordinary practitioners of Kalachakra are currently meditating in Tibet. Unfortunately, conditions in Tibet make it difficult for international students to meet and learn from these yogis. For this reason, Rinpoche is working hard to construct an International Kalachakra Retreat Center in the hills above Dzamthang Tsangwa Monastery. His vision is to create a space where generations of students from all over the world can come to receive rare transmissions and to practice within the incredible blessings of the region. Eventually, Rinpoche hopes these same students will then convey those blessings to the rest of the world.

The Collected Works of Khentrul Rinpoche

https://khentrulrinpoche.com/about/bibliography/

The Realm of Shambhala
A Complete Vision for Humanity's Perfection

(2021)

The Great Middle Way
Clarifying the Jonang View of Other-Emptiness

(2020)

Unveiling Your Sacred Truth through the Kalachakra Path
Book One: The External Reality — Book Two: The Internal Reality
Book Three: The Enlightened Reality

(2017)

Hidden Treasure of the Profound Path
A word-by-word commentary on the Kalachakra Preliminary Practices

(2016)

Ocean of Diversity
An unbiased summary of views and practices,
gradually emerging from the teachings of the world's wisdom traditions

(2015)

A Happier Life
How to develop genuine happiness and wellbeing
during every stage of your life

(2014)

www.ingramcontent.com/pod-product-compliance
Lightning Source LLC
Chambersburg PA
CBHW071203070526
44584CB00019B/2898